My
Excel® 2013

Michael Alexander

que®

800 East 96th Street,
Indianapolis, Indiana 46240 USA

My Excel® 2013

Copyright © 2013 by Que Publishing

ISBN-13: 978-0-7897-5075-4
ISBN-10: 0-7897-5075-9

Library of Congress Cataloging-in-Publication Data is on file and available upon request.

Printed in the United States of America

First Printing: May 2013

Trademarks

All terms mentioned in this book that are known to be trademarks or service marks have been appropriately capitalized. Que Publishing cannot attest to the accuracy of this information. Use of a term in this book should not be regarded as affecting the validity of any trademark or service mark.

Warning and Disclaimer

Every effort has been made to make this book as complete and as accurate as possible, but no warranty or fitness is implied. The information provided is on an "as is" basis. The author and the publisher shall have neither liability nor responsibility to any person or entity with respect to any loss or damages arising from the information contained in this book.

Bulk Sales

Que Publishing offers excellent discounts on this book when ordered in quantity for bulk purchases or special sales. For more information, please contact

U.S. Corporate and Government Sales

1-800-382-3419

corpsales@pearsontechgroup.com

For sales outside of the U.S., please contact

International Sales

international@pearsoned.com

Editor-in-Chief
Greg Wiegand

Executive Editor
Loretta Yates

Development Editor
Charlotte Kughen

Managing Editor
Kristy Hart

Senior Project Editor
Lori Lyons

Copy Editor
Apostrophe Editing Services

Indexer
Tim Wright

Proofreader
Dan Knott

Technical Editor
Laura Acklen

Editorial Assistant
Cindy Teeters

Book Design
Anne Jones

Compositor
Bronkella Publishing

Contents at a Glance

	Introduction	**xi**
Chapter 1	Working with Excel's Ribbon Menus	**3**
Chapter 2	Managing Workbooks and Worksheets	**15**
Chapter 3	Entering and Managing Data	**31**
Chapter 4	Formatting Worksheet Data	**53**
Chapter 5	Working with Formulas and Functions	**89**
Chapter 6	Working with Charts	**133**
Chapter 7	Working with Graphics	**153**
Chapter 8	Printing in Excel	**173**
Chapter 9	Working with Pivot Tables	**195**
Chapter 10	Using SkyDrive to Store and Share Excel Files	**215**
Appendix A	Excel Shortcut Keys	**227**
	Index	**231**

Table of Contents

Introduction   **xi**

1   **Working with Excel's Ribbon Menus**   **3**

     Familiarizing Yourself with the Ribbon Tabs 4

     Understanding Workbooks and Worksheets 7

         Explore Worksheets 7

         Explore Columns, Rows, and Cells 8

     Understanding Contextual Tabs 9

         Work with Contextual Tabs 10

     Customizing the Quick Access Toolbar 10

         Add a Command to the Quick Access Toolbar 11

         Add Other Commands to the Quick Access Toolbar 12

         Add Hidden Commands to the Quick Access Toolbar 13

2   **Managing Workbooks and Worksheets**   **15**

     Opening an Excel Workbook 16

     Closing an Excel Workbook 17

     Saving a Workbook 17

     Switching Between Open Workbooks 18

     Switching Between Worksheets 20

     Viewing Multiple Workbooks 20

     Inserting and Deleting Worksheets 22

     Renaming Worksheets 23

     Coloring Worksheet Tabs 23

     Moving Worksheets Within a Workbook 24

     Copying Worksheets Between Workbooks 25

     Password Protect a Workbook 26

     Protecting a Worksheet 28

3   **Entering and Managing Data**   **31**

     Entering Data 32

     Editing and Deleting Existing Data 33

Zooming into Your Data...34

Undoing and Redoing Changes.....................................35

Copying and Pasting Data...36

    Cut and Paste Data...37

Freezing Rows and Columns...38

Splitting a Worksheet...39

Inserting Cells...40

Deleting Cells..41

Inserting and Deleting Rows...42

Inserting and Deleting Columns....................................43

Moving Data..44

Finding Data...46

Replacing Data..47

Applying a Data Filter..48

Sorting Data..49

Adding and Managing Cell Comments...........................50

4 Formatting Worksheet Data   53

Changing the Font and Font Size...................................54

Changing Column Width...55

Changing the Color of the Cell Background and Cell Text....57

Formatting the Display of Numeric Data........................58

    Use a General Format...60

    Use a Number Format..61

    Use a Currency Format...62

    Use a Date Format...63

    Use a Text Format..64

Applying Bold, Italic, and Underline..............................65

Using Merge and Center on Cells..................................66

Changing Horizontal Data Alignment.............................68

Changing Row Height...69

Changing Vertical Data Alignment.................................70

Changing Cell Orientation...71

Wrapping Data in a Cell...72

Changing Borders..72

Indenting Entries in a Cell..73

Clearing Formatting 74

Hiding and Unhiding Rows 76

Hiding and Unhiding Columns 78

Hiding and Unhiding a Worksheet 80

Using Format as Table 81

Copying Formatting 82

Creating and Applying a Formatting Style 84

Using Conditional Formatting 85

5   Working with Formulas and Functions   89

Using AutoSum Calculations 89

    Find a Cell Average (AVERAGE) 91

    Find the Largest Cell Amount (MAX) 92

    Find the Smallest Cell Amount (MIN) 93

    Count the Number of Cells (COUNT) 94

Entering a Formula 95

Editing a Formula or Function 96

Copying a Formula 97

Assigning Names to a Cell or Range 99

Referencing Names in a Function 100

Using Functions Across Worksheets 101

Using Auto-Calculate 104

Finding and Using Excel Functions 105

    Calculate a Loan Payment (PMT) 107

    Perform a Logical Test Function (IF) 110

    Conditionally Sum a Range (SUMIF) 113

    Find the Future Value of an Investment (FV) 115

Recognizing and Fixing Errors 118

    Fix the #DIV/0! Error 119

    Fix the #NAME? Error 120

    Fix the #VALUE! Error 122

    Recognize the #REF! Error 124

Recognizing Circular References 126

Checking for Formula References (PRECEDENTS) 128

Checking for Cell References (DEPENDENTS) 130

6 **Working with Charts**   **133**

Creating a Chart 134

Changing the Chart Type 136

Altering the Source Data Range 137

Altering Chart Options 138

Formatting the Plot Area 142

Formatting the Chart Area 144

Formatting the Axis Scale 146

Altering the Original Data 147

Adding Data to Charts 149

Adding a Legend 150

7 **Working with Graphics**   **153**

Using Drawing Tools 153

Inserting Clip Art 156

Inserting a Picture from File 157

Using AutoShapes 158

Inserting WordArt 160

Using Smart Art in Excel 161

Inserting a Diagram 163

Inserting Objects 164

Working with Inserted Objects 166

    Format an Object 167

    Move an Object 168

    Resize an Object 170

    Delete an Object 171

8 **Printing in Excel**   **173**

Using Print Preview 174

Setting the Print Area 175

Adjusting Page Margins 177

Inserting Page Breaks 178

Working in Page Break Preview Mode 181

Printing a Worksheet on One Page 182

Printing in Portrait or Landscape Orientation 184

Centering a Worksheet on a Page 185

Printing Gridlines and Row/Column Headers 186

Printing Cell Comments 187

Printing Cell Error Indicators 188

Printing Repeating Row and Column Titles 189

Adding Headers and Footers 190

Printing Your Worksheets 191

9 Working with Pivot Tables **195**

Creating a Pivot Table 196

Rearranging a Pivot Table 199

Adding a Report Filter 201

Refreshing Pivot Table Data 203

Adding Pivot Table Data 204

Customizing Field Names 206

Applying Numeric Formats to Data Fields 207

Changing Summary Calculations 209

Showing and Hiding Data Items 210

Sorting Your Pivot Table 211

10 Using SkyDrive to Store and Share Excel Files **215**

Signing Up For SkyDrive 215

Signing into SkyDrive 217

Saving a Workbook to SkyDrive 218

Opening a SkyDrive Workbook 220

Downloading a Workbook from SkyDrive 222

Sharing Your SkyDrive Workbooks with Others 223

Managing SkyDrive Workbooks 224

A Excel Shortcut Keys **227**

Using the Excel Shortcut Key Reference Table 227

Index **231**

About the Author

Michael Alexander has been named a Microsoft MVP for his ongoing contributions to the Excel community. A Microsoft Certified Application Developer (MCAD), he has authored several books on advanced business analysis with Excel and Access, including *Easy Microsoft Excel 2010*. He has 15+ years' experience developing Office solutions, and runs the free Excel and Access tutorial and tips site datapigtechnologies.com.

Dedication

For my family.

Acknowledgments

Thank you, Geoff.

We Want to Hear from You!

As the reader of this book, *you* are our most important critic and commentator. We value your opinion and want to know what we're doing right, what we could do better, what areas you'd like to see us publish in, and any other words of wisdom you're willing to pass our way.

We welcome your comments. You can email or write to let us know what you did or didn't like about this book—as well as what we can do to make our books better.

Please note that we cannot help you with technical problems related to the topic of this book.

When you write, please be sure to include this book's title and author as well as your name and email address. We will carefully review your comments and share them with the author and editors who worked on the book.

Email: feedback@quepublishing.com

Mail: Que Publishing
         ATTN: Reader Feedback
         800 East 96th Street
         Indianapolis, IN 46240 USA

Reader Services

Visit our website and register this book at quepublishing.com/register for convenient access to any updates, downloads, or errata that might be available for this book.

Introduction

Welcome to the world of Excel. Okay, that's a bit cheesy. But if you look around the business world, the financial world, the manufacturing world, and any other industry you can think of, you see people using Excel. Excel is everywhere. It is by far the most-used program in the history of business applications. So in a real way, there is truly a world of Excel. This is probably why you picked up this book. You need a way to accelerate your learning and get up to speed in Excel.

Well, worry not, dear reader. Whether you're boning up on Excel for a new job (congratulations, by the way), a school project, or just for home use, this book is perfect for you. *My Excel 2013* provides concise, visual, step-by-step instructions for the most-common tasks you need to do in Excel. You won't be inundated with fancy descriptions of every little function and feature. It quickly gets right to the core tasks you need to start. You learn how to create, edit, format, and print worksheets, as well as how to create charts and use Excel formulas. Just about everything you need to get up and running with Excel is in this one easy book.

What's in This Book

First, you explore the user interface. You get a sense of where to choose tasks, where to enter information, and how to move around in Excel. From there, you find out how to manage your Excel files. This includes creating new Excel workbooks, saving workbooks, and moving worksheets between workbooks.

Next, you explore the various methods for getting data into Excel. You also walk through some techniques that enable you to manage and more easily work with the data in your Excel worksheets.

You continue with the topic of formatting data. Here, you discover how to make your workbook your own by adding colors and applying fonts. You also find out how to make your data more readable by applying number formatting and cell formatting.

After you cover the basics, the book gives you a solid introduction to Excel functions and formulas. First, you see how to create and implement your own formulas. Then, you get tutorials on how to use the most commonly used Excel functions.

Next, you explore charting in Excel. Here, you get an understanding of how to create charts in Excel and how to customize them to fit your needs. From there, you continue to discover some of the ways you can add graphics and other visualizations into your Excel worksheets.

Printing is the last topic in your introduction to Excel. Although printing sounds trivial, Excel has many print options you can use to configure your workbooks to print properly.

For those of you preparing for a corporate job, Chapter 9 introduces you to the topic of pivot tables. One of the most-useful features in Excel, pivot tables enables any Excel analyst to analyze large amounts of data with just a few clicks.

You round out your tour of Microsoft Excel with an exploration of Microsoft's SkyDrive platform, where you can save, view, and edit your Excel documents on the Web.

After going through all the topics covered in this book, you can say that you know how to use Excel!

Quick Access toolbar

Tabs

Command buttons

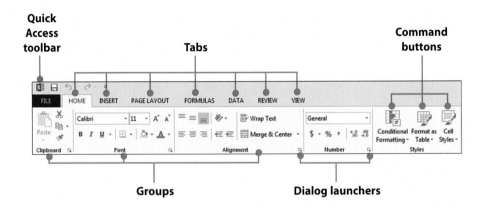

Groups

Dialog launchers

In this chapter, you are introduced to Excel's Ribbon menu and learn the basics of working with workbooks and worksheets. Topics covered in this chapter include

→ Familiarizing yourself with the Ribbon tabs
→ Understanding contextual tabs
→ Understanding workbooks and worksheets
→ Customizing the Quick Access Toolbar

Working with Excel's Ribbon Menus

Like any other application, Excel has a basic workspace called the user interface. A user *interface* is the combination of screens, menus, and icons you use to interact with an application. In Excel, the user interface is primarily composed of the Ribbon menu, workbooks, and worksheets. The Ribbon is the name given to the row of tabs and buttons you see at the top of Excel. The Ribbon's tabs and buttons bring your favorite commands into the open by showing multiple commands grouped in specific categories.

The Ribbon is made up of five basic components: the Quick Access Toolbar, tabs, groups, command buttons, and dialog launchers.

- The **Quick Access Toolbar** is essentially a customizable toolbar to which you can add commands that you use most frequently.

- **Tabs** contain groups of commands that are loosely related to core tasks. Actually, it helps to think of each tab as a category.

- **Groups** contain sets of commands that fall under the umbrella of that tab's core task. Each group contains buttons, which you click to activate the command you want to use.

- **Dialog launchers** are activated by clicking the small arrow located in the lower-right corner of certain groups. Clicking any dialog launcher activates a dialog box containing all the commands available for a given group.

Familiarizing Yourself with the Ribbon Tabs

Each tab on the Ribbon contains groups of commands loosely related to a central task. Don't be alarmed by the number of commands on each tab. As you go through this book, you'll quickly become familiar with each of the common Excel commands. For now, take some time to become familiar with each of Excel's default tabs (the way they are set up before you customize it to fit your working needs).

1. Click the Home tab. This tab contains commands for common actions such as formatting, copying, pasting, inserting, and deleting columns and rows.

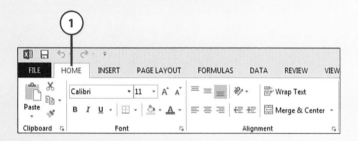

2. Click the Insert tab. This tab contains commands that enable you to insert objects such as charts and shapes into your spreadsheets.

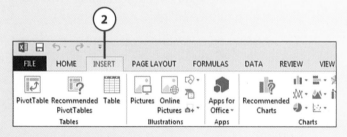

3. Click the Page Layout tab. This tab holds all the commands that enable you to determine how your spreadsheet looks, both onscreen and when printed. These commands control options such as theme colors, page margins, and print area.

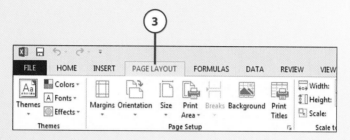

4. Click the Formulas tab. This tab holds all the commands that help define, control, and audit Excel formulas.

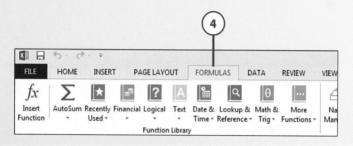

5. Click the Data tab. This tab features commands that enable you to connect to external data, as well as manage the data in your spreadsheet.

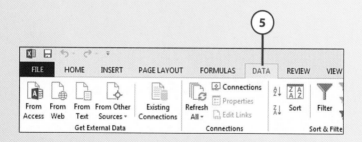

6. Click the Review tab. With commands such as Spell Check, Protect Sheet, Protect Workbook, and Track Changes, the theme of the Review tab is protecting data integrity in your spreadsheet.

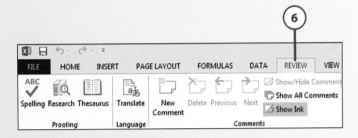

7. Click the View tab. The commands on this tab are designed to help you control how you visually interact with your spreadsheet.

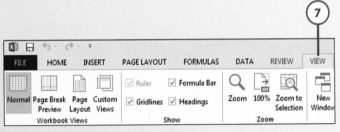

8. The File tab exposes the Backstage view, where you find commands to help you open existing Excel workbooks, create new workbooks, save workbooks, apply protection, and much more. Chapter 2, "Managing Workbooks and Worksheets," covers the File tab in detail.

Minimizing the Ribbon

If you feel the Ribbon takes up too much space at the top of your screen, you can minimize it—that is to say, you can hide the Ribbon and show only the tab names. To do this, simply right-click the Ribbon and select Unpin the Ribbon. At this point, the Ribbon becomes visible only if you click on a tab. To revert back to the default Ribbon view, right-click the Ribbon, and click the Unpin the Ribbon toggle.

Understanding Workbooks and Worksheets

An Excel file, often referred to as a *workbook*, contains one or more spreadsheets, or *worksheets*. Each box in the worksheet area is referred to as a *cell*. Each cell has a *cell address*, which is composed of a *column reference* and a *row reference*. The letters across the top of the worksheet make up the column reference. The numbers down the left side of the worksheet make up the row reference. For example, the address of the top, leftmost cell is A1. This is because the cell is located at the intersection of the A column and row 1.

By default, Excel 2013 opens a new workbook with one blank worksheet. You can add, delete, and rename worksheets within a workbook, as needed.

Explore Worksheets

1. Open Excel and open a new Blank workbook.

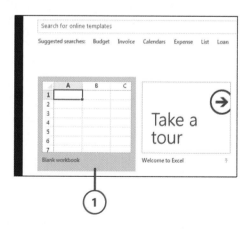

2. The workbook opens with one worksheet called Sheet1. This worksheet contains cells you can use to start entering and editing data.

3. Click the plus icon to add a new worksheet.

4. The new worksheet is added and named Sheet2. Each time you add a worksheet, Excel gives the worksheet a default name of Sheet XX, where XX is the next sequential number.

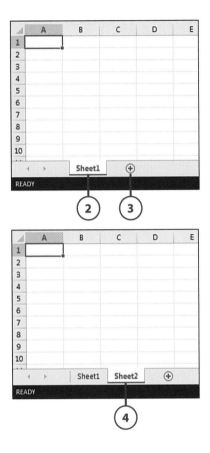

Workbooks and Worksheets in Depth

You read more about managing workbooks and worksheets in detail in Chapter 2.

Explore Columns, Rows, and Cells

1. Click the column reference and observe how the entire column is selected.

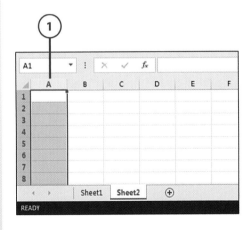

2. Click the row reference and observe how the entire row is selected.

3. Click the cell intersecting at column A and row 1. You can select a single cell on the worksheet area.

The Big Grid

Excel 2013 has 1,048,576 rows and 16,384 columns. This means that there are more than 17 billion cells in a single Excel worksheet. So what happens if you need more than 1 million rows and more than 16,000 columns? Well, the short answer is that you'll have to start a new worksheet.

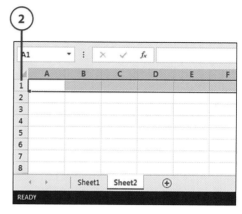

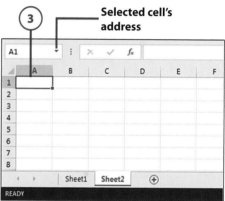

Selected cell's address

Understanding Contextual Tabs

Contextual tabs are special types of tabs that appear only when a particular object is selected, such as a chart or a shape. These contextual tabs contain commands specific to whatever object you are currently working on.

For example, after you add a shape to a spreadsheet, a new Format tab appears. This is not a standard tab, but a *contextual* tab—meaning it activates only when you work with a shape.

Follow the steps in this task to add a shape and view the contextual tab.

Work with Contextual Tabs

1. Open Excel and start a new blank workbook (as described earlier in the "Explore Worksheets" task). When the new workbook is open, click the Insert tab.

2. Click the Shapes command button.

3. Click the rectangle shape in the menu of shapes.

4. Click anywhere on your spreadsheet to embed your selected shape.

All Shapes and Sizes
Read more about shapes and other graphics in Chapter 7, "Working with Graphics."

---

5. Click your new shape to select it, and you see the contextual tab, labeled Format, that appears any time the shape is selected.

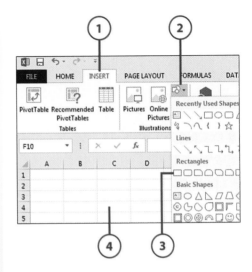

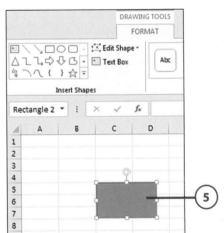

Customizing the Quick Access Toolbar

The small buttons at the top-left side of the Excel screen are known collectively as the Quick Access Toolbar. By default, the Quick Access Toolbar contains three commands: Save, Undo, and Redo. If you click the drop-down selection arrow next to the Redo button on the Quick Access Toolbar, you see that these 3 commands are only 3 of 11 available as prebuilt or built-in options. Placing a check next to any of the options that you see here automatically adds each option to the Quick Access Toolbar. So, clicking New adds the New command, and clicking Open adds the Open command. You can actually click each one of these and have all 11 options available to you in the Quick Access Toolbar. In the tasks that follow, you find out how to add commands to the Quick Access Toolbar to customize it to fit your workflow.

Add a Command to the Quick Access Toolbar

Follow these steps to add to the Quick Access Toolbar one of the commands available from the drop-down menu.

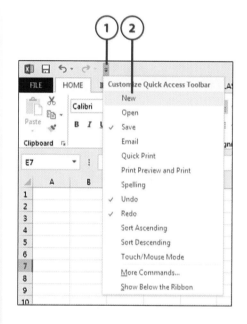

1. Click the arrow to open the Quick Access toolbar drop-down to see all the existing commands you can add.

2. Click the New command to add it to the Quick Access toolbar.

3. You now have a New icon on your Quick Access toolbar.

Moving the Quick Access Toolbar

You can move the Quick Access Toolbar under the Ribbon by right-clicking its drop-down arrow and selecting Show Below the Ribbon. This moves the entire Quick Access Toolbar under the Ribbon—closer to your worksheet.

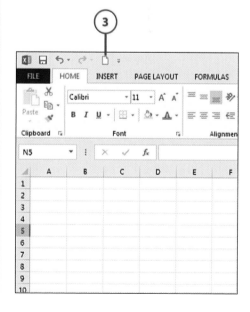

Add Other Commands to the Quick Access Toolbar

You're not limited to only the commands available on the Quick Access Toolbar drop-down menu—you can add all kinds of commands. For example, if you often work with shapes, you can add the Shapes command to the Quick Access Toolbar.

1. Click the Insert tab.

2. Right-click the Shapes command button.

3. Click the Add to Quick Access Toolbar menu item.

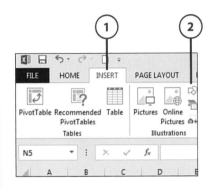

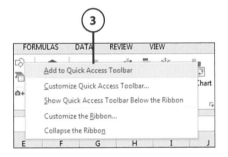

Adding Entire Groups

You can add entire groups to your Quick Access Toolbar. For instance, if you often use the Illustrations group on the Insert tab, you can right-click that entire group and select the Add to Quick Access Toolbar option.

Add Hidden Commands to the Quick Access Toolbar

A closer look at the drop-down menu next to the Quick Access Toolbar reveals an option called More Commands. When you click this item, the Excel options dialog box opens up with the Quick Access Toolbar panel activated. This panel enables you to select from the entire menu of Excel commands, adding them to your Quick Access Toolbar. This comes in handy if you want to add some of the more obscure Excel commands that aren't found on the Ribbon.

1. Click the Quick Access Toolbar drop-down arrow.

2. Select the More Commands option.

3. Choose Commands Not in the Ribbon.

4. Find and select the AutoFilter command.

5. Click the Add button.

6. Click OK to add the command to the Quick Access Toolbar.

Removing Commands

To remove a command from the Quick Access Toolbar, simply right-click it and select the Remove from Quick Access Toolbar option.

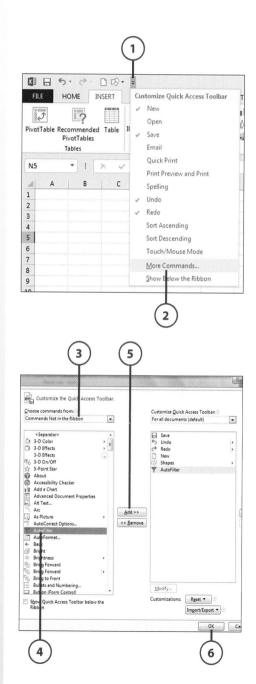

Click the File tab
and enter the
Backstage view

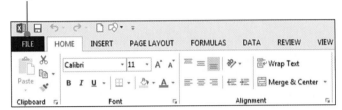

Use the commands in the Backstage view
to print, save, and manage your Excel files

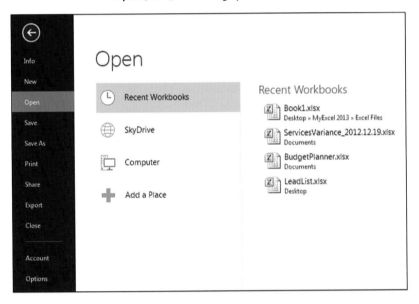

This chapter covers some of the more fundamental tasks you undertake in Excel; tasks that revolve around managing your workbooks and worksheets. The topics covered in this chapter include

- → Opening and closing an Excel workbook
- → Saving a workbook
- → Switching between workbooks
- → Viewing multiple workbooks
- → Organizing and customizing worksheets
- → Password protecting a workbook
- → Protecting a worksheet

Managing Workbooks and Worksheets

A workbook is essentially a container that holds your worksheets. When people refer to an Excel workbook, they are referring to the entire Excel file. A worksheet is the actual spreadsheet you work in. There can be many worksheets in a workbook—similar to pages in a book.

Excel 2013 includes a File tab. The File tab exposes the Backstage view. In the Backstage view you find every command you need to manage and work with Excel workbooks. The more common tasks found are opening Excel workbooks, creating new workbooks, and saving workbooks. The Backstage view also provides options to share files, see file information, and access Excel application options.

Opening an Excel Workbook

Any time you want to work with an existing Excel workbook, first you must open it. The idea here is simple: First you tell Excel you want to open a file, and then you select the file you want using the Open dialog box.

1. Click the File tab.

2. Click the Open command.

3. Select the location in which your file resides.

4. Click the Browse icon to browse your chosen location.

5. Use the Open dialog box to find the file you want to open and then double-click the file.

6. Excel opens the workbook. The filename displays at the top of the workbook.

Creating a New Workbook

If you want to start a new workbook from scratch, you can click the File tab, select New, and then select Blank Workbook. Alternatively, you can go to your keyboard and press the shortcut key combination Ctrl+N.

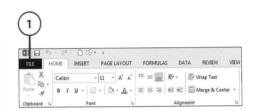

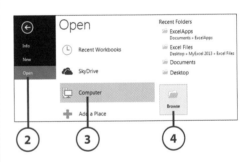

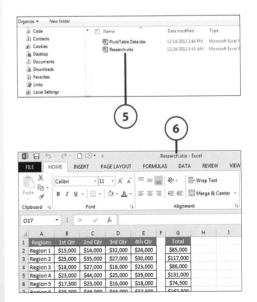

Closing an Excel Workbook

Excel 2013 introduces the concept of one workbook—one window. That is to say, each workbook you open has its own window. This makes it easier to work with multiple workbooks at one time. This comes in handy when you work on two monitors. When closing a workbook, the entire Excel window closes. This is a departure from Excel's previous behavior of closing the workbook but keeping the Excel window open.

1. Click the Close button (represented by the X) in the document window. If you've made changes to the workbook, Excel prompts you to save your changes.

2. Click Save if you want to save any changes you have made, or click Don't Save if you do not. Excel responds accordingly and then closes the workbook.

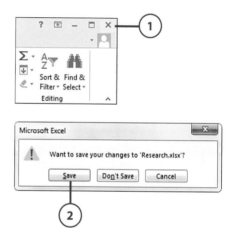

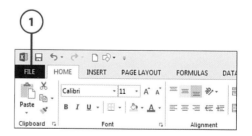

Saving a Workbook

You should regularly save your workbooks as you work in them so you don't lose data. You can save a workbook as many times as you like, so saving often is a good habit to get into. You can also save your workbook under another name if you want to keep track of multiple versions of your workbook.

1. Click the File tab to get to the Backstage view.

2. Click the Save As command.

3. Choose the location you want your file saved.

4. Click the Browse button to locate the folder where you want to save the file.

5. Use the Save As dialog box to enter a new name for your file.

6. Click the Save button, and Excel saves your workbook.

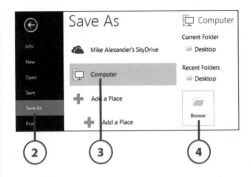

Clicking Save on the Quick Access Toolbar

If you have already saved and named your file, you can resave it after making additional changes by clicking the Save icon on the Quick Access Toolbar. Revisit Chapter 1, "Working with Excel's Ribbon Menus," for a refresher on the Quick Access Toolbar.

Switching Between Open Workbooks

You can have multiple workbooks open at the same time and switch between them whenever you want. For example, you might be using two different workbooks to create one report. You can use the Windows Taskbar to quickly move from one workbook to another.

1. With two or more workbooks already open, hover over the Excel icon on the Windows Taskbar.

2. Click the button on the Windows Taskbar that represents one of your open workbooks (in this case, the Excel2013.xlsx button). This workbook becomes the active workbook.

3. Click a different workbook button on the Windows Taskbar (for instance, the Excel2013DataLists.xlsx button). This workbook becomes the active workbook.

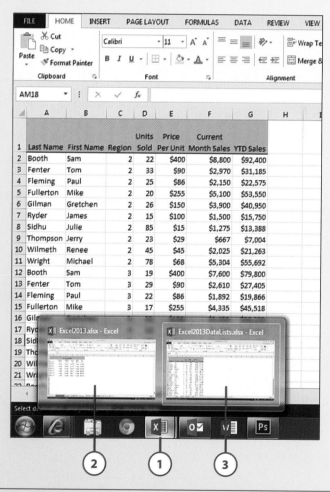

Using Alt+Tab to Toggle Through Workbooks

You can also toggle through your open workbooks by using the Windows Alt+Tab toggle. With several workbooks open, you can press the shortcut key Alt+Tab. This enables you to cycle through all the open applications/workbooks and stop on the workbook you want.

Switching Between Worksheets

Similar to switching between multiple workbooks, you can switch between the separate worksheets within a single workbook. This enables you to review and edit data stored on separate worksheets within a single workbook.

1. Click a worksheet tab (in this example, the Sheet1 tab) to see the contents in that worksheet.

2. Click a different worksheet tab (here, the Sheet2 tab) to see the contents of that worksheet.

Cycle Through Sheets with the Keyboard

You can also cycle through the sheets in your workbook with keyboard combinations. Press Ctrl+PgUp to go to the next sheet. Press Ctrl+PgDown to go to the previous sheet.

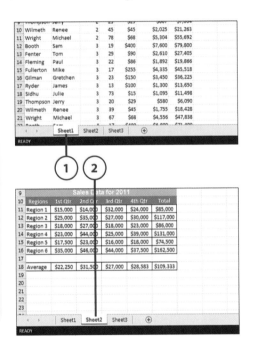

Viewing Multiple Workbooks

Instead of constantly switching between workbooks, you can view multiple workbooks onscreen in Excel and resize their windows as needed. This comes in handy if you want to compare two or more workbooks or work on multiple workbooks at the same time.

1. Click the View tab, and then select the Arrange All command.

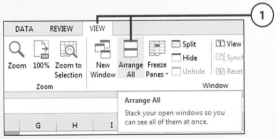

2.   Select how you want the windows arranged (for example, Horizontal).

3.   Click the OK button.

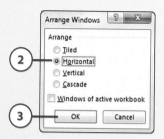

4.   Multiple workbooks display simultaneously. Click the title bar or in the body of the workbook you want to work in to make it the active worksheet.

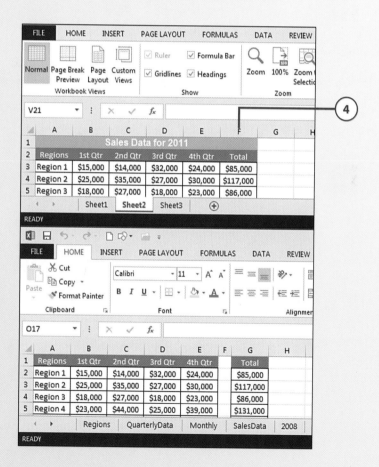

Vertical or Horizontal

If you need to compare two workbooks where the data is column-oriented (data is mostly going up and down) use the Vertical option when arranging the window. If you need to compare two workbooks where the data is row-oriented (data is mostly left to right) use the Horizontal option.

Inserting and Deleting Worksheets

By default, Excel automatically provides you with one worksheet when a new workbook is created. As you work with Excel, you can likely find that you need to insert additional worksheets. Conversely, sometimes you need to delete ones you no longer use.

1. To insert a new worksheet, click the plus icon next to the worksheet tabs.

2. The new worksheet is automatically named SheetX, where X is the next number in the sequence of sheets.

3. To delete a worksheet, right-click the worksheet tab you want to delete.

4. Click the Delete command.

5. Click the Delete button to confirm that you want to delete the worksheet.

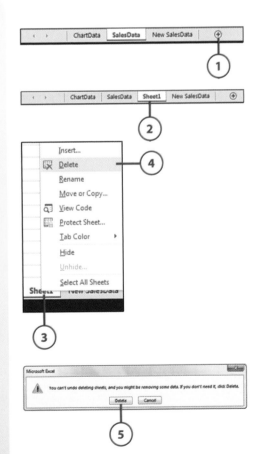

No Undo When Deleting Worksheets

Be careful when deleting worksheets because there is no way to undo after you delete a worksheet. If you mistakenly delete a sheet, there is no way to get it back.

Renaming Worksheets

You should always endeavor to use descriptive names for the worksheets in your Excel file. If you have a workbook that uses multiple worksheets, providing descriptive names for your worksheets makes working within your workbook far easier than it would be if all your sheets are named Sheet1, Sheet2, and so on.

1. Double-click the worksheet tab you want to rename. Alternatively, you can right-click the worksheet name and select Rename.

2. Type the new name and press Enter. Excel displays the new name on the worksheet tab.

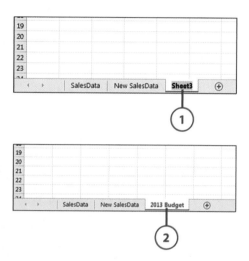

Worksheet Names Can't Be Too Long

Excel has a 31-character limit on worksheet names. That is, your worksheets cannot have a name that exceeds 31 characters.

Coloring Worksheet Tabs

As you add worksheets to your workbook, you might find an increasing need to organize your worksheets. To help with this, Excel enables you to color your worksheet tabs. If you want to indicate something specific about a worksheet tab—for example, if a worksheet contains preliminary data—you can assign it a tab color, such as red.

1. Right-click the worksheet tab you want to color.

2. Click Tab Color.

3. Select your preferred color.

4. The color is immediately applied to your worksheet tab.

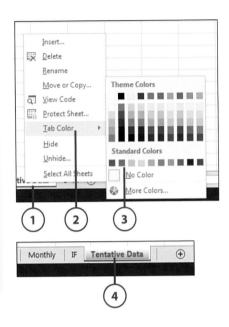

Moving Worksheets Within a Workbook

When Excel inserts a new worksheet, it always places it in front of the currently selected worksheet. You can, of course, move your worksheet tabs as you start organizing your workbook.

1. Right-click the worksheet tab that you want to move.

2. Select Move or Copy from the shortcut menu. The Move or Copy dialog box opens.

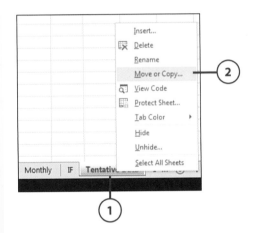

3. In the list of worksheets, click the name of the worksheet in front of which you want the selected sheet to be moved.

4. Click OK to move the worksheet.

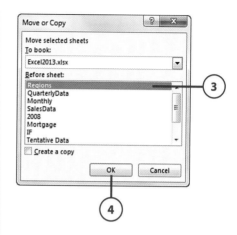

Move by Dragging

You can also click a worksheet tab and drag it in front of or after another worksheet tab to change its location. This can be a much more efficient method of moving worksheets in smaller workbooks that contain only a handful of worksheets.

Copying Worksheets Between Workbooks

You might find that a worksheet used in one workbook would be of use in another workbook. Instead of re-creating the worksheet, you can simply create a copy of the worksheet in the other workbook.

1. Right-click the worksheet tab that you want to copy.

2. Select Move or Copy from the shortcut menu. The Move or Copy dialog box opens.

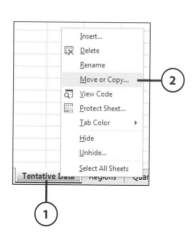

3. Click the down arrow next to the To Book field, and choose the workbook to which you want the target worksheet copied.

4. Choose the position where you want the worksheet copied. Click the Create a Copy check box.

5. Click OK. At this point, Excel copies the worksheet as directed.

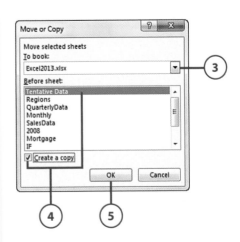

Moving Versus Copying

Be sure to click the Create a Copy option when copying a worksheet. If you fail to do so, the worksheet is moved to the other workbook instead of copied. If the worksheet is moved, it is no longer accessible in the current workbook.

Password Protect a Workbook

You might have instances in which your Excel workbooks are so sensitive that only certain users are authorized to see them. In these cases, you can force your workbook to require a password to open.

1. With your workbook open, click the File tab to get to the Backstage view.

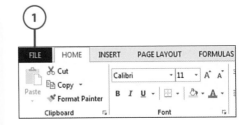

2. Click the Protect Workbook drop-down, and select the Encrypt with Password option.

3. Enter an appropriate password and then click OK.

4. Enter the same password in the Reenter Password box and then click OK. At this point, your worksheet is protected.

Remember Your Passwords

Excel offers no way to recover lost or forgotten passwords. You must remember them.

If you lose or forget your password, you have to use a third-party password-hacking program. You can find dozens of them by going to your favorite Internet search engine and entering "Excel Lost Password."

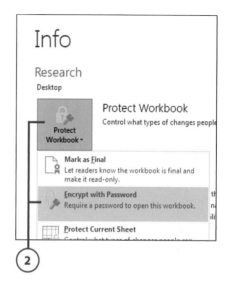

Protecting a Worksheet

When you share files with other users, you might find it useful to protect your worksheets. When your worksheet is protected, you essentially restrict the capability to take certain actions without a password—actions such as inserting or deleting rows and cell data.

1. Go to the Review tab and select the Protect Sheet command.

2. Place a check mark next to the actions that you want users to perform, and then enter a password in the Password to Unprotect Sheet text box.

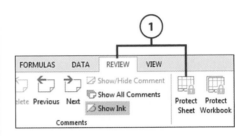

3. Click OK.

4. Type the same password in the Confirm Password dialog box; then click OK. At this point, your worksheet is protected.

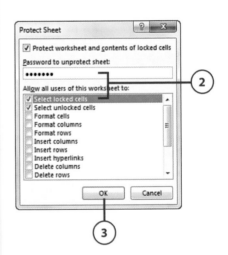

The Password Is Optional

If you leave the Password entry blank, your worksheet is still protected. However, your users can unprotect the worksheet without a password.

5. To unprotect a worksheet, go to the Review tab, and select the Unprotect Sheet command. The Unprotect Sheet dialog box appears.

6. Enter the password.

7. Click OK. At this point, the worksheet is unprotected.

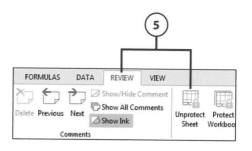

Excel Passwords are Case Sensitive

Be aware that passwords are case-sensitive in Excel. That is, if you enter the password as "RED" (uppercase letters), your worksheet can't be unprotected if you enter "red" in lowercase letters.

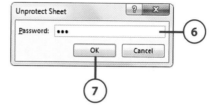

Check spelling

Undo changes

Redo changes

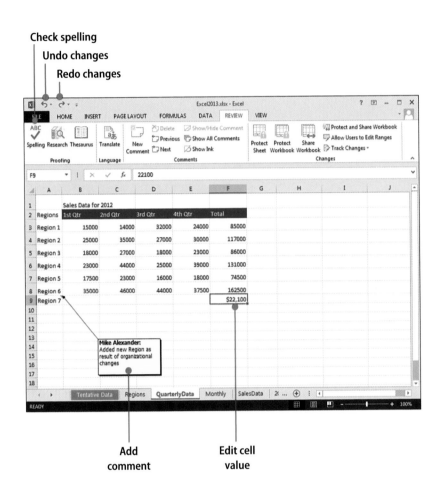

Add comment

Edit cell value

In this chapter, you explore the mechanics of entering, editing, and managing data in Excel. The topics covered here include

→ Entering and editing data
→ Copying and pasting data
→ Working with rows and columns
→ Splitting a worksheet
→ Working with cells
→ Finding, moving, and replacing data
→ Filtering and sorting data

3

Entering and Managing Data

Data is the technical term for the text and numbers you enter into an Excel worksheet. Each cell in an Excel worksheet can contain data made up of text, numbers, or any combination of both.

The capability to make changes to the values in your worksheet is what makes Excel such a valuable analysis tool. You can insert a cell, row, or column. You also can delete or change entries, find and replace data, and even check for spelling errors. In addition to editing the data in your worksheets, you can add comments to remind yourself of information.

Entering Data

The quickest and easiest way to get data into Excel is to enter the data via the keyboard. You can enter data into a blank worksheet or add data to an existing worksheet. For example, you can enter the word **Fruits** in cell A2 and press the Enter key.

1. Click the cell you want to edit, making it active.

2. Enter some data (in this case, Fruits) in the cell. As you type, the data also displays on the Edit bar.

3. Press Enter when your edit has been made. Excel makes the cell below (the one you just edited) the active cell.

4. Enter some data into a few different cells, pressing the arrow keys to move around.

Correcting Data While Editing

If you make a mistake while entering data, simply press the Backspace key to delete all or a portion of your entry and enter the correct data.

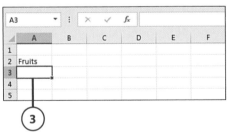

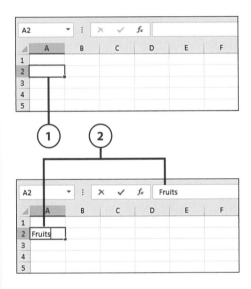

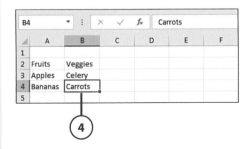

Editing and Deleting Existing Data

You can always replace a cell's contents with new data. This comes in handy when you need to correct typing errors or when a cell contains the wrong data. You can also easily erase the contents of a cell by using the Delete key. Erasing a cell is useful when you change your mind about the contents after you enter the data in the cell.

1. Double-click the cell you want to edit.

2. Edit the portion of data you need changed.

3. To delete a value, click the target cell.

4. Press Delete on your keyboard.

Use Your Arrow Keys

You can press the left and/or right arrow keys on your keyboard to move the insertion point where you want to make changes.

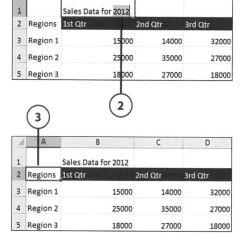

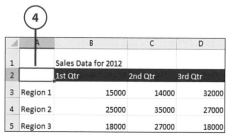

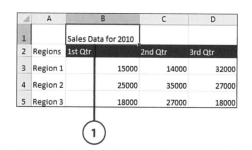

Zooming into Your Data

If you want to zoom in and get a closer look at data in your worksheet, you can select a higher percentage of magnification. On the other hand, if you want to zoom out so that more of the worksheet shows on the screen at one glance, select a lower percentage of magnification. Excel 2013 provides several ways to zoom in and out.

1. Slide the Zoom Slider in the lower-right corner of Excel. Watch your worksheet increase and reduce in magnification as you slide.

   Or

2. To zoom in on a specific area of the worksheet, select a range of cells, and then click the View tab. Select a Range and choose the Zoom to Selection command. Excel automatically increases or reduces magnification so that only that selection is visible.

   Or

3. Select the Zoom command on the View tab to open the Zoom dialog box. Choose your wanted magnification. After you click OK, observe how Excel applies your zoom preference.

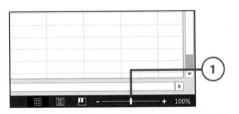

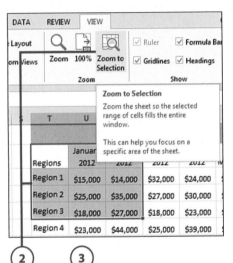

Zoom with Your Mouse Wheel

If you have a mouse wheel (a wheel in the center of your mouse between the left and right buttons) you have another quick way to zoom. Hold down the Ctrl key on your keyboard while you spin your mouse wheel. This increases or reduces magnification depending on the direction you spin (up or down).

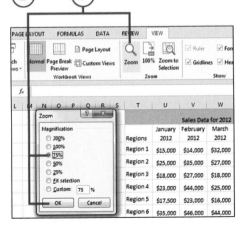

Undoing and Redoing Changes

If you make a mistake while working on your spreadsheet and you detect your error immediately, you can undo your action. In addition, if you undo an action by mistake, you can use Excel to quickly redo it. Excel keeps track of your actions in the Undo/Redo Stack. The Undo/Redo Stack holds up to 100 of your last actions.

1. Click the Undo icon on the Quick Access Toolbar to undo your most-recent action.

2. Click the drop-down button next to the Undo icon to undo all actions to a certain point.

3. Click the Redo icon on the Quick Access Toolbar to redo your most recent action.

4. Click the drop-down button next to the Redo icon to redo all actions to a certain point.

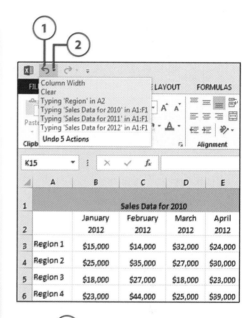

Using Keyboard Shortcut Keys

A quick and easy way to undo an action is to use the Ctrl+Z shortcut. Press and hold down the Ctrl key while pressing the Z key. You can redo an action using the Ctrl+Y shortcut.

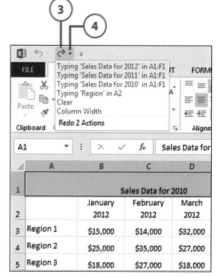

Copying and Pasting Data

You can avoid the trouble of retyping duplicate information in a worksheet by cutting or copying data from one part of a worksheet to another. For example, if you need to duplicate a column of data, there is no need to retype that data. You can copy the data and paste it where you need it.

1. Click the first cell in the range you want to copy, and then drag down to highlight the entire range.

2. Click the Copy button on the Home tab.

3. Click the cell to which you want the range to be pasted.

4. Click the Paste button on the Home tab. Excel duplicates your range.

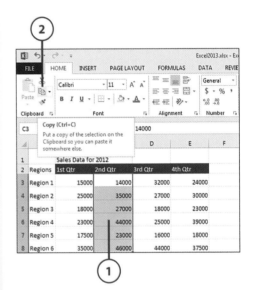

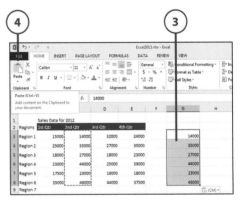

Cut and Paste Data

You can also cut and paste data. When you cut and paste, you remove data from one part of your worksheet and paste it in another part. For example, if you want to move a column, you can cut it from its location and paste it to a new location.

1. Click the first cell in the range you want to copy, and then drag down to highlight the entire range.

2. Click the Cut button on the Home tab.

3. Click the cell to which you want the range to be pasted.

4. Click the Paste button on the Home tab. Excel moves your range.

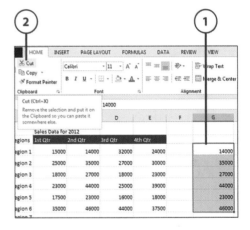

Using Keyboard Shortcut Keys

A quick and easy way to copy and paste data is to use the Ctrl+C and Ctrl+V shortcuts. Press and hold down the Ctrl key while pressing the C key to copy. Then hold down the Ctrl key while pressing the V key to paste. To cut and paste, you can use the Ctrl+X and Ctrl+V shortcut key combinations.

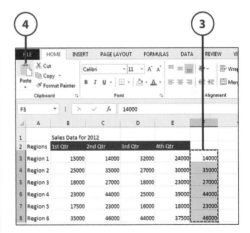

Freezing Rows and Columns

You might create worksheets that are so large that you cannot view all your data on the screen at the same time. In addition, if you have added row or column labels and you scroll down or to the right, you'll lose sight of your labels and which data field you're reviewing. For example, if you are reviewing sales data in columns E and F, it would be nice to see the row title of the cells you are referencing. To help, you can *freeze* the heading rows and columns so that they're always visible.

1. Click in the cell below the row you want to freeze.

2. On the View tab, click the Freeze Panes command.

3. Click Freeze Top Row. At this point, you can scroll down and still see the first row of your data table.

4. To unfreeze the panes, go back to the Freeze Panes command, and click the Unfreeze Panes command.

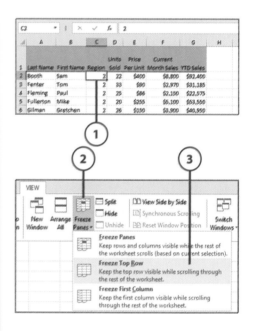

Freezing a Column

If you are freezing a column, click the cell to the right of the column you want to freeze. Then follow the steps outlined here, but select the **Freeze First Column** command.

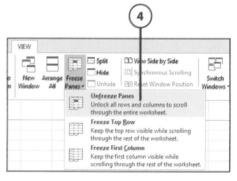

Splitting a Worksheet

By *splitting* a worksheet, you can scroll independently into different horizontal and vertical parts of a worksheet. This is useful if you want to view different parts of a worksheet or copy and paste between different areas of a large worksheet.

1. Click in the cell where you want to split the worksheet.

2. On the View tab, click the Split command. You see a split bar separating your worksheet into two independently scrollable sections.

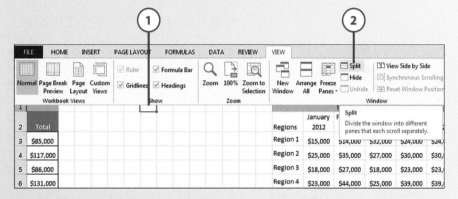

3. Move through the worksheet to see how easily you can simultaneously view other parts of the worksheet.

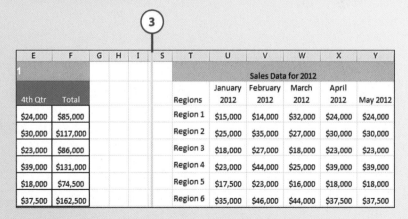

Removing Split Bars

To remove the split bars, click the Split command on the View tab.

Inserting Cells

There might be times when you need to insert new cells into the middle of your dataset. For example, if you have a table that shows data by region, you might need to insert blank cells to accommodate a new region. To avoid retyping all the data or copying and pasting, you can insert cells and shift the current cells to their correct locations.

1. Select the cell or cells that need to be shifted to insert new cells.

2. Right-click and choose the Insert option.

3. Choose whether you want to shift existing cells right or down to make room for the new cells. Then click OK.

4. Click in your newly created cells and start adding data.

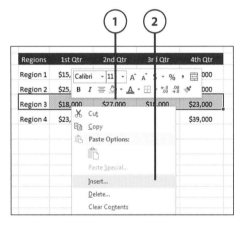

It's Not All Good

Watch for Misaligned Data

Be aware that when you insert a cell, the cells below or to the right of that cell shift (one row down or one column to the right). When this happens, make certain that your data table does not become misaligned. That is, be careful that the data that is shifted does not need to remain with its original row or column to make a complete record. If it does, you might want to use the Insert Rows or Insert Columns options (explained in the sections "Inserting and Deleting Rows" and "Inserting and Deleting Columns").

You need to be similarly careful when you delete a cell because the cells below or to the right of that cell shift (one row up or one column to the left). If the data that shifts needs to stay with its original row or column, you might want to use the Delete Rows or Delete Columns options, which are also explained later in this chapter.

Deleting Cells

As you work with worksheets, you might find that data needs to be eliminated to keep the worksheet up to date. You can easily delete extraneous cells and shift existing cells to their correct locations.

1. Select the cell or cells that need to be deleted.

2. Right-click and choose the Delete option.

3. Choose whether you want to shift existing cells left or up to fill the empty space left by the deleted cells. Click OK.

4. Observe that Excel has deleted the specified cells.

Regions	1st Qtr	2nd Qtr	3rd Qtr	4th Qtr
Region 1	$15,000	$14,000	$32,000	$24,000
Region 2	$25,000	$35,000	$27,000	$30,000
Region 4	$23,000	$44,000	$25,000	$39,000

Inserting and Deleting Rows

You can insert extra rows into a worksheet to make more room for additional data or formulas. Adding more rows, which gives the appearance of adding space between rows, can also make the worksheet easier to read. Alternatively, you can delete rows from a worksheet to close up some empty space or remove unwanted information.

1. Right-click the row number of the existing row where you want to insert a new row.

2. Click the Insert option. Excel automatically adds a new row.

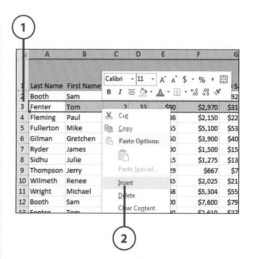

3. To delete a row, right-click the row number of the existing row that you want to delete.

4. Click the Delete option. Excel automatically removes the specified row.

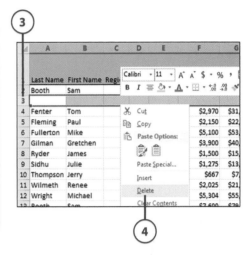

HIDE ROWS INSTEAD OF DELETE ROWS

>>>Go Further

If you feel there might be a chance that you will need the rows you are deleting, another alternative is to leave them intact—only hidden. That is to say, you can hide them by selecting your rows, right-clicking, and then selecting the Hide option. This way, the rows are not visible, but you can always get them back by unhiding them. To unhide, select the rows above and below the hidden rows, right-click, and then select the Unhide option.

Inserting and Deleting Columns

You will often need to add another column of data to your worksheets. In these cases, you can insert columns. Alternatively, you might want to delete columns from a worksheet to remove data you no longer need.

1. Right-click the column letter of the existing column where you want to insert a new column.

2. Click the Insert option. Excel automatically adds a new column.

3. To delete a column, right-click the column number of the existing column that you want to delete.

4. Click the Delete option. Excel automatically removes the specified column.

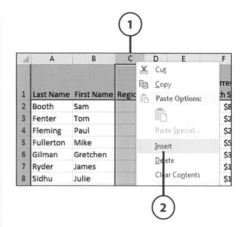

Hide Columns Instead of Delete Columns

You can always hide your columns instead of deleting them for good. This way, you can always get them back simply by unhiding them. It's easy to do. Select the columns you want to hide, right-click, and then select the Hide option. To unhide, select the columns to the left and right of the hidden columns, right-click, and then select the Unhide option.

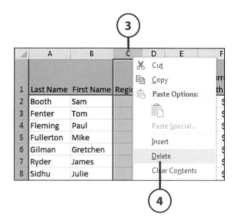

Moving Data

Excel gives you the option to move data with a simple click and drag of the mouse. If you hate taking your hands off the mouse, the simplicity of this action might appeal to you.

1. Select the cells you want to move.

2. Click the border of the selected cells to drag the cells to the location in the worksheet where you want to move the data.

3. Observe that Excel has moved your data.

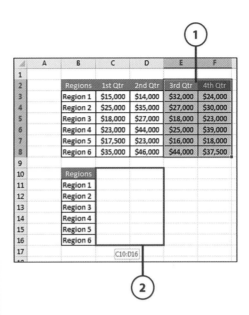

Moving Versus Cutting and Pasting

Moving data is essentially the same action as cutting and pasting data. That is, both actions enable you to move large chunks of data from one location to another. But you would typically "move" data when you need to move the data a short distance and don't want to take your hand off the mouse. You would usually employ cut and paste when you need to move your data large distances or to another worksheet or workbook.

Finding Data

You will often encounter situations in which you need to find specific information in a large spreadsheet. For example, suppose you want to quickly find the row that shows the sales information for Jerry Thompson. Instead of scanning each row for the data you need, which can be time-consuming, you can use Excel's Find feature.

1. On the Home tab, click Find and Select.

2. Click Find.

3. Enter the data you want to find in the Find What text box.

4. Click the Find Next button. Excel finds the first instance of the data you typed and makes the cell that contains it the active cell. You can click the Find Next button to search for the next instance.

5. Click Close when you finish searching.

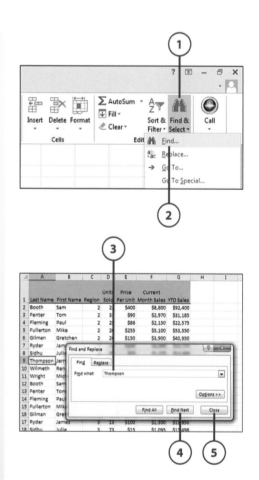

Finding All Instances

Click the Find All button in the Find and Replace dialog box to view a list—complete with cell locations and worksheet tab names—of all the instances of the data you entered in the Find What text box. While there, you can press Ctrl+A to have Excel select all the cells in that list.

Shortcut to Find

As with most tasks in Excel, you can employ a quick shortcut key combination to call up the Find dialog box. Press Ctrl+F to quickly go to the Find dialog box.

Replacing Data

Imagine that you discover some data in your table in which a company's name has been consistently misspelled, or that a salesperson you reference in a data table has changed his last name. You definitely would not want to find and replace all that data manually. Fortunately, Excel enables you to search for instances of incorrect or outdated data and replace it with new data using its Find and Replace feature.

1. On the Home tab, click Find and Select and then click Replace. The Find and Replace dialog box appears.

2. In the Find What text box, type the data you would like to find. Press the Tab key to move the cursor to the Replace With text box, and type the replacement data.

3. Click Replace All to replace all instances of the data you typed. (Alternatively, click Find Next to find the first instance of the data, and click Replace to replace it.)

4. Excel notifies you of the number of replacements it made. Click OK.

Narrowing Your Search Criteria

Clicking the Options button on the Find and Replace dialog box reveals a few options you can use to make search criteria more specific. To conduct a case-sensitive search (for example, finding all instances of "Thompson" but not "thompson"), choose the Match Case option. Choose Match Entire Cell Contents to limit your search to cells that contain no more and no less than the data you type.

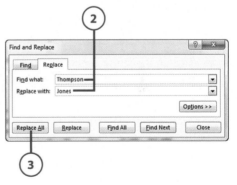

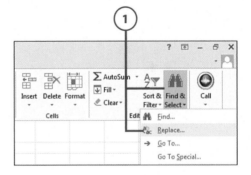

Applying a Data Filter

When working with a large data table, it is sometimes useful to filter the table so that you can see or work only with a specific set of records. For instance, say you want to see only the sales reps in Region 2. When you want to work with a subset of records, you can use Excel's Filter. The Filter function enables you to see only those records that meet the criteria you select.

1. Click the Filter button on the Data tab. You immediately see filter drop-downs inside each of your header columns.

2. Click the drop-down selector for the column you want to filter.

3. Click the (Select All) option to clear all the check boxes, and then click the check box next to the value by which you want to filter. Click OK to apply the filter.

4. Observe that all the filtered row numbers are blue, which indicates a filtered state.

Removing Data Filter Drop-Downs

To remove the data filter drop-downs, simply go to the Data tab and click the Filter button. This clears all filters and eliminates the drop-downs from your header labels.

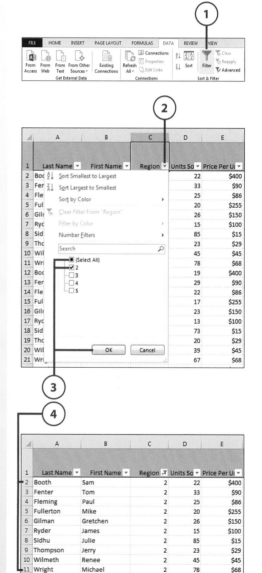

Sorting Data

You will often want to change the ordering of your data. For example, you might want to sort a table of sales reps by their regions and then by YTD sales. You can meet this need by using Excel's Sort function.

1. Click any cell within the data table you are going to sort.

2. On the Data tab, click the Sort command.

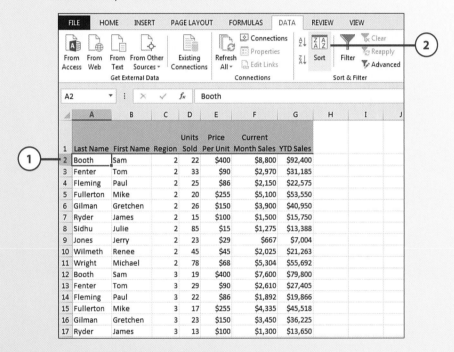

3. The Sort Dialog box opens. Select the field you want to sort, and then specify whether you want to sort Smallest to Largest or Largest to Smallest.

4. Click the Add Level button to add another level of sorting.

5. Select another field to sort by, and then specify whether you want to sort Smallest to Largest or Largest to Smallest.

6. After you click OK, Excel immediately applies your custom sort.

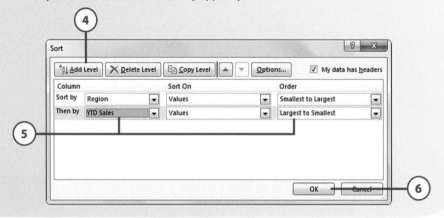

Adding and Managing Cell Comments

Some cells contain data that requires an explanation or special attention. Comments provide a way to attach this type of information to individual cells without cluttering the cells with extraneous information. A red triangle indicates that a cell contains a comment, which you can view in several different ways. After a comment is in place, Excel makes it easy to edit or delete it.

1. Right-click the cell to which you want to add a comment.

2. Select Insert Comment.

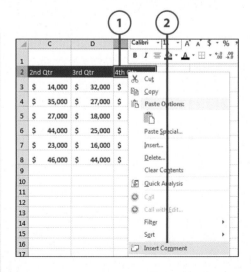

3. Type the wanted text into the comment area. When you finish, click anywhere in the worksheet to accept the comment.

4. The cell's upper-right corner now contains a red triangle, indicating the presence of a comment. To view the comment, hover the mouse pointer over the triangle.

Display Comments Without Hovering

You can make Excel display a cell's comments without the need to hover over the cell. To do so, right-click the commented cell, and select Show/Hide Comments. To rehide the comment, right-click the commented cell and select Hide Comment.

5. To edit a comment, right-click the commented cell.

6. Select the Edit Comment option.

7. To delete a comment, right-click the commented cell.

8. Select the Delete Comment option.

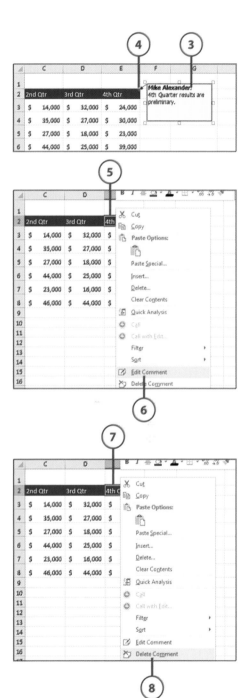

Vertical alignment

Alignment of text to top of cell

Cell background color

Underline

Font colors

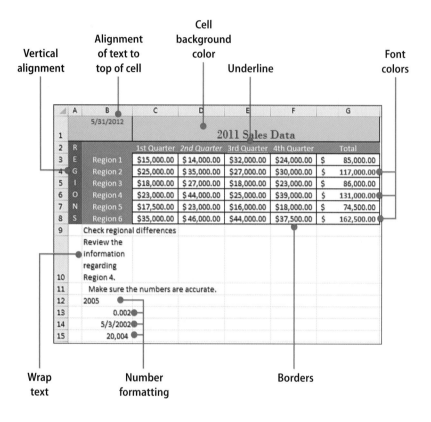

Wrap text

Number formatting

Borders

In this chapter, you explore the various types of formatting you can apply to both your cells and your data. The topics in this chapter include

→ Changing the font, font size, and font style
→ Changing column width and row height
→ Changing the background and text color
→ Modifying data alignment and cell orientation
→ Changing borders
→ Clearing and copying formatting
→ Hiding rows, columns, and worksheets
→ Using Format as Table
→ Creating and applying a formatting style
→ Using conditional formatting

Formatting Worksheet Data

The primary purpose of Excel's formatting tools is to make your worksheet more readable. For example, you can change the display of the numbers so that they don't contain decimal places. This enables your audience to see the needed data without being inundated with superfluous numbers.

Excel's formatting options can be partitioned into two buckets: cell formatting and data formatting.

Cell formatting changes the look and feel of the cells. For instance, you can change the cell background colors, add borders, change alignment, add underline or bold effects to cell contents, and wrap text.

Data formatting changes the data to the most readable and appropriate way. For example, you can format a number to show as currency complete with the dollar symbol. Or you can format a date so that is shows as Jan-14 instead of 01/01/2014.

Changing the Font and Font Size

One way to format data in your worksheet is to change the font used to display it. This gives data a different look and feel, which can help differentiate the type of data a cell contains. You can also change the font's size for added emphasis.

1. Select the cells whose font and font size you want to change, or click the All Cells button (to the left of column A and above row 1) to format all the cells in the worksheet.

2. Click the Font field down arrow on the Home tab, and scroll through the available fonts. When you find the one you want to use, click it to select it.

Finding Font Names

If you know the name of the font you want to apply, select the down arrow next to the Font field, and type the first letter of the font name. You are immediately moved to the portion of the list that starts with the typed letter.

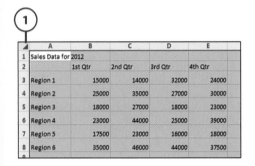

3. Click the Font Size field down arrow and scroll through the available sizes (in points). When you find the size you want to use, click it to select it.

4. Note that the font and font size you selected are applied.

Formatting Options

To format only a portion of a cell's data, select only that portion and then change the font. You can also select a font (or other options) before you begin typing, and all the data in that cell appears with the selected font or options.

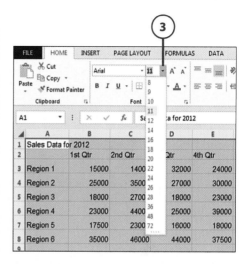

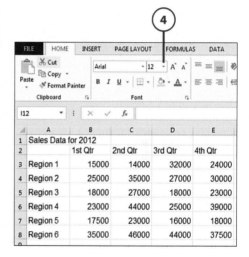

Changing Column Width

There might be times when data is too wide to display within a cell, particularly if you just applied formatting to it. Excel provides several alternatives for fixing this problem. You can select columns and specify a width or force Excel to automatically adjust the width of a cell to exactly fit its contents.

1. Move the mouse pointer over one side of the column header; then click and drag the column edge to the wanted width. (The column size displays in the Name box.)

2. To resize multiple columns simultaneously, select the columns that you want to alter.

3. Click and drag one of the selected columns' header edges to the wanted width and release it.

4. All the selected columns are resized to the same width.

Quick AutoFit Column Widths

Here's a quick and easy way to automatically make all columns fit their individual contents. Select the columns you want to alter, move the cursor over the right side of the column header, and double-click when the cursor changes to a two-headed arrow. Your columns automatically snap tightly around their contents.

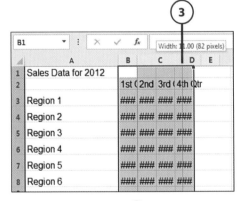

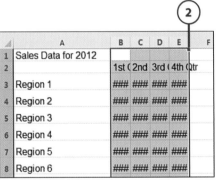

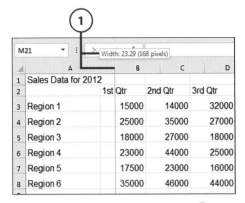

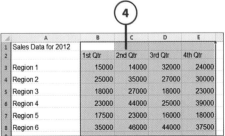

Changing the Color of the Cell Background and Cell Text

Generally, cells present a white background for displaying data, but you can apply other colors or shading to the background. You can even combine these colors with various patterns for a more attractive effect. In addition, you can change the color of the data contained within your worksheet's cells.

1. Select the cells whose background color and/or font color you want to change.

2. To change the color of the text in the selected cells, click the Font Color down arrow on the Home tab, and choose a color from the list (here, white).

3. To change the color of the selected cells' background, click the Fill Color down arrow, and choose a color from the list (here, blue). Excel applies the colors.

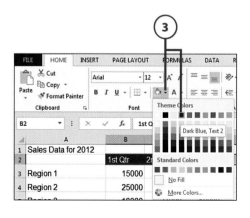

Choosing Colors

Be sure a shading or color pattern doesn't interfere with the readability of your data. To improve readability, you might need to make the text bold or select a text color that goes well with your cells' background color.

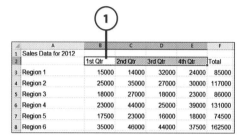

Think of the Printer

If you print the worksheet to a non-color printer, the color you select prints gray—and the darker the gray, the less readable the data. Yellows generally print as a pleasing light gray that doesn't compete with the data.

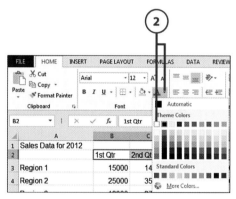

Formatting the Display of Numeric Data

You can alter the display of different numbers depending on the type of data the cells contain. By formatting numeric data, you can display data in a familiar format to make it easier to read. For example, sales numbers can display in a currency format, and scientific data can display with commas and decimals.

1. After you select the cells you want to format, click the Increase Decimal command on the Home tab twice (once for each decimal place you want displayed).

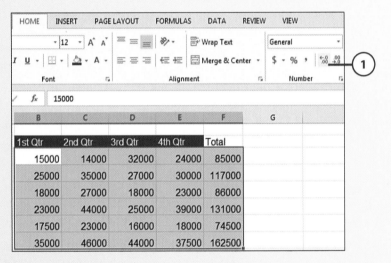

2. Click the Comma Style command on the Home tab to add a comma to the numeric data.

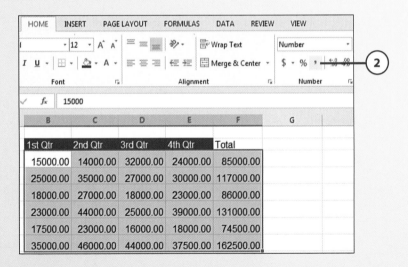

3. Click the Accounting Number Format command on the Home tab to format numbers in the selected cells with a dollar sign ($), commas, a decimal point, and two decimal places.

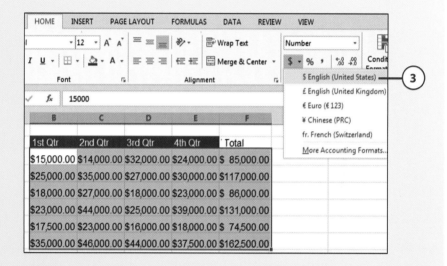

Percent Style

If you click the Percent Style command on the Home tab, your numbers convert to a percentage and display with a % symbol.

Handling the #### Error

After you apply a style to cells, if any cells display the error ########, it simply means that the data in the cell exceeds the current cell width. Refer to the task "Changing Column Width" in Chapter 2, "Managing Workbooks and Worksheets," to fix the problem.

Use a General Format

When you enter numbers into Excel cells, the General format is the default. No specific number format (discussed in the next task) is applied. The General format is used when you record counts of items, increment numbers, or do not require any particular format. If you have applied another format to your cells but want to return to this default General format, follow the steps in this task.

1. After you select the cells you want to format, click the down arrow in the Number Format drop-down box (on the Home tab).

2. Click the General option in the Category list.

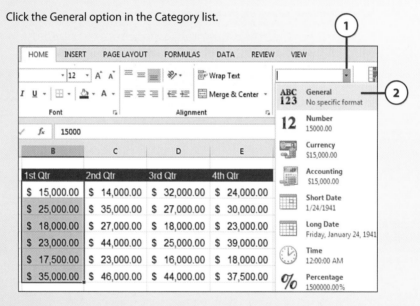

3. Excel changes the format.

Use a Number Format

When you apply the Number format in Excel, it uses two decimal places by default. You have the option to alter the number of decimal places, use a comma separator, and even determine the way you want negative numbers to appear (for example, with a minus sign, in red, in parentheses, or some combination of the three).

1. After you select the cells you want to format, click the down arrow in the Number Format drop-down on the Home tab.

2. Click the Number option in the Category list.

3. Excel changes the format.

Quickly Increase and Decrease Decimal Places

In the Number group on the Home tab are the Increase Decimal and Decrease Decimal commands. These commands enable you to quickly change the number of decimal places used in your values.

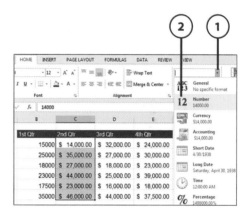

Use a Currency Format

When you apply the Currency format in Excel, it uses two decimal places and a dollar sign by default. You have the option to alter the number of decimal places, display a symbol for a different currency, and even determine the way you want negative numbers to appear.

1. After you select the cells you want to format, click the down arrow in the Number Format drop-down box on the Home tab.

2. Click the Currency option in the Category list.

3. Excel changes the format.

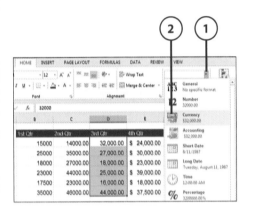

Currency Format Options

Use the Decimal Places field in the Number tab of the Format Cells dialog box to change the number of decimal places used. To choose a different currency symbol, select it from the Symbol drop-down list.

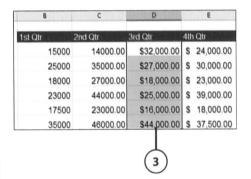

Currency-Related Formats

The Accounting format automatically lines up the currency symbols and decimal points for the cells in a column. The Percentage format multiplies the cell value by 100 and displays the result with a percent symbol.

Use a Date Format

When you apply the Date format in Excel, it displays the date and time serial numbers as date values. There are numerous date types you can assign to your dates. For example, you might find it easier to skim through dates as numbers with or without the assigned year visible. Or perhaps you would rather use the actual name of the month (as opposed to a numeral) for reference.

1. After you select the cells you want to format, go to the Home tab, and click the down arrow in the Number Format drop-down box.

2. Click the Short Date option in the Category list.

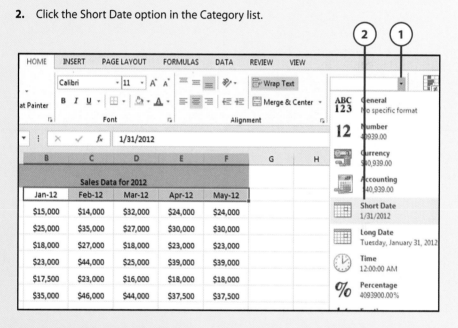

3. Excel changes the format.

Using Time and Custom Formats

You can use the Time format if you want to display just the time (not the date) in your spreadsheet. In addition, you can use the Custom format option (in the Format Cells dialog box) to create your own Date and Time format.

Use a Text Format

When you type numeric data into a cell, the display defaults to a Number format. When you apply the Text format in Excel, it displays numbers as text regardless of whether the data in the cell is numeric or text-based. This can be convenient when you want to enter a number that isn't meant to be calculated or used in a mathematical operation. For example, you might need to enter a customer number that has leading zeros. Formatting this number as text ensures that the leading zeroes remain visible.

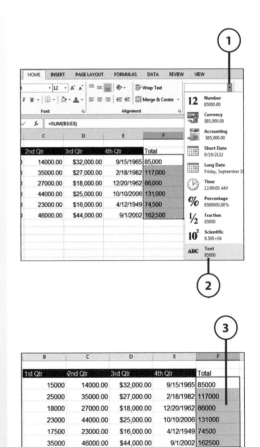

1. After you select the cells you want to format, click the down arrow in the Number Format drop-down box (on the Home tab).

2. Click the Text option in the Category list.

3. Excel changes the format.

Immediate Number Text

Another way to immediately make a number a textual cell entry is to type an apostrophe (') before you type the number. This tells Excel that the number is to be treated as text.

Applying Bold, Italic, and Underline

You can format the data contained in one or more cells as bold, italic, or underlined (or some combination of the three) to draw attention to it or make it easier to find. Indicating summary values, questionable data, or any other cells is easy with this type of formatting.

1. Select the cells in which you want to apply bold formatting, and click the Bold command.

2. Select the cells in which you want to apply italic formatting, and click the Italic command.

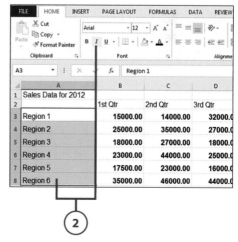

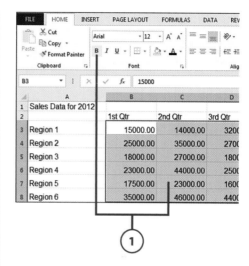

3. Select the cells in which you want to apply underline formatting, and click the Underline command.

4. The bold, italic, and underlining are applied to the selected cells.

Combination Formatting

You can use several formatting techniques in combination, such as applying bold, italic, and underlining at the same time. Simply select the text you want to format, and click each of the commands on the Home tab.

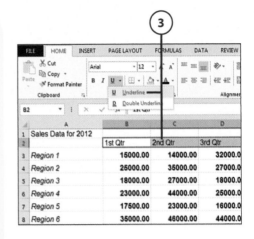

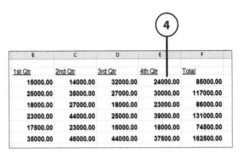

Using Merge and Center on Cells

Using Excel's Merge and Center feature, you can group similar data under one heading. Columns of data usually have column headers, but they can also have group header information representing multiple columns.

1. Select the cells you want to merge, including the cells that don't contain any data.

2. Click the Merge and Center command on the Home tab.

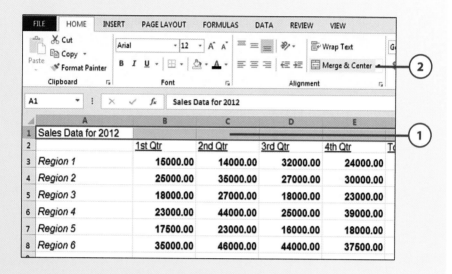

3. The cells in the group header are merged, and the data is centered. Repeat the steps in this task as needed to group additional columns in your worksheet.

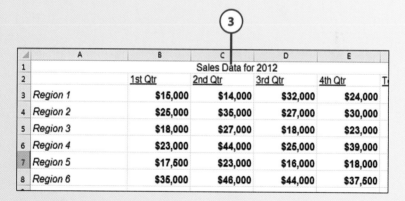

Unmerging Cells

To unmerge or separate cells that have been merged, place your cursor in the merged cell; then go to the Home tab and click the Merge and Center command.

Changing Horizontal Data Alignment

Excel provides several ways to format data, and one way is to align it. The most common alignment changes you make will probably be to center data in a cell, align data with a cell's right edge (right-aligned), or align data with a cell's left edge (left-aligned). The default alignment for numbers is right-aligned; the default alignment for text is left-aligned.

1. Select the cells in which you want to align the data to the left, and click the Align Left command on the Home tab.

2. Select the cells in which you want to align the data to the right, and click the Align Right command.

3. Select the cells in which you want to center the data, and click the Center command.

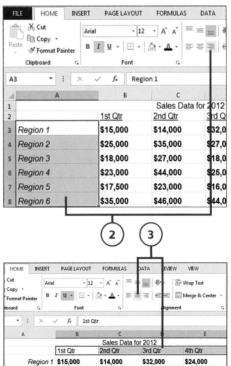

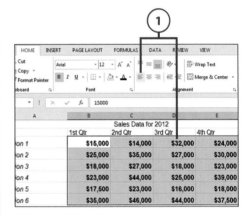

4. The alignments are applied to the selected cells.

Changing Row Height

Depending on the formatting changes you make to a cell, data might not display properly. Increasing the font size or forcing data to wrap within a cell might prevent data from being entirely displayed or cause it to run over into other cells. You can frequently avoid these problems by resizing rows.

1. Move the mouse pointer over the bottom edge of the row header. Click and drag the row to the wanted height; the row size displays in the bubble.

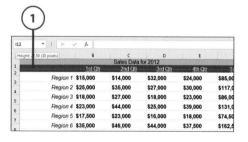

2. To resize multiple rows simultaneously, select the rows you want to alter.

3. Click and drag one of the selected row's bottom edges to the wanted height and then release it. All the selected rows are resized to the same height.

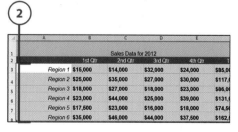

Quick AutoFit Rows

Here's a quick and easy way to automatically make all rows fit their individual contents: Select the rows you want to alter; then move the cursor over the top border of any of the row numbers, and double-click when the cursor changes to a two-headed arrow. Your rows automatically snap tightly around their contents.

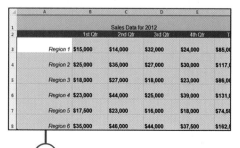

Changing Vertical Data Alignment

In addition to aligning the data in your cells horizontally, you can align your cell data in a vertical format. Perhaps you want the data in your cells to align to the top of the cell, the bottom of the cell, or the center of the cell, or you want the data to justify within the cell. Cell data defaults to the bottom of the cell, but you can change this according to the look you want.

1. Select the cells in which you want to align the data.

2. Go to the Home tab, and click the Middle Align command.

3. The data is vertically aligned within the cell.

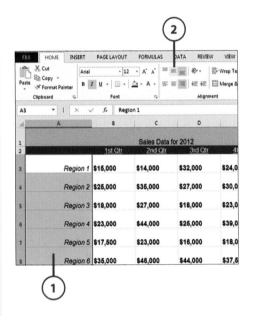

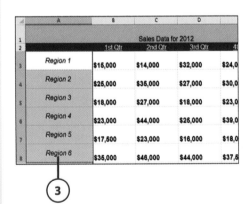

Changing Cell Orientation

Excel enables you to alter the orientation of cells—that is, the angle at which a cell displays information. The main reason for doing this is to help draw attention to important or special text. This feature can be convenient when you have a lot of columns in a worksheet and you don't want your column headers to take up much horizontal space, or if you simply want the information to stand out.

1. After you select the cell or cells whose orientation you want to change, click the Orientation command in the Alignment group on the Home tab.

2. Choose Angle Counterclockwise (shown here) or Angle Clockwise.

3. The data reorients within the cell. (You might need to increase or decrease the height and width of the cells.)

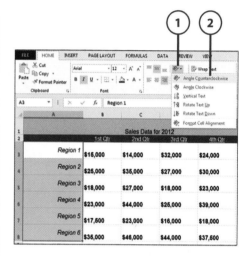

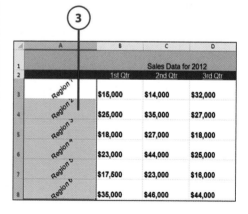

More Control over Rotating Data

Although the Orientation command gives you an easy way to alter the orientation of your cells, you might need a bit more control over the angle of the orientation. You can define your own orientation angles by right-clicking any cells and selecting Format Cells. In the Format Cells dialog box that appears, go to the Alignment tab. There you see a section called Orientation containing a half-circle. You can rotate the text in the target cell by clicking the red dot there and dragging it to the wanted angle.

Wrapping Data in a Cell

Another way to format data is to allow text to wrap in a cell. For example, suppose a heading (row or column, for example) is longer than the width of the cell holding the data. If you want to make your worksheet organized and readable, it is a good idea to wrap the text in the heading so that it is completely visible in a cell.

1. After you select the cell or cells whose text you want to wrap, click the Wrap Text command in the Alignment group on the Home tab.

2. The data in the selected cells is automatically wrapped and the cell height adjusts.

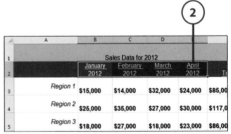

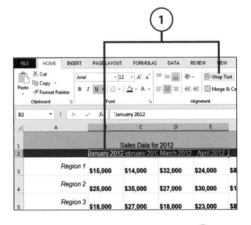

Aligning Wrapped Text

You might need to alter the column width to have the data wrap at the location you want. You also can align data that has been wrapped, which gives your text a cleaner look. Refer to the tasks "Changing Horizontal Data Alignment" and "Changing Vertical Data Alignment" earlier in this chapter to learn how to align data in cells.

Changing Borders

Each side of a cell is considered a border. Borders provide a visual cue as to where a cell begins and ends. You can customize borders to indicate other beginnings and endings, such as grouping similar data or separating headings from data. For example, a double line is often used to separate a summary value from the data being totaled. Changing the bottom of the border for the last number before the total accomplishes this effect.

1. Select the cells to which you want to add some type of border.

2. On the Home tab click the down arrow next to the Borders command, and then choose an option from the list that appears—for example, All Borders.

3. The border is applied.

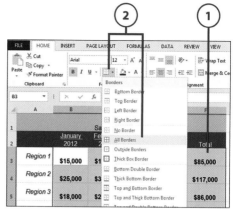

Removing Borders

To remove a border, select the bordered cells, click the down arrow next to the Borders command, and choose the No Border option from the list that appears.

Indenting Entries in a Cell

Another alignment option you might want to use is to indent entries within a cell. Doing so can show the organization of entries—for example, subcategories of a budget category.

1. After you select the cell or range whose data you want to indent, click the Increase Indent command the number of times you want the entries indented.

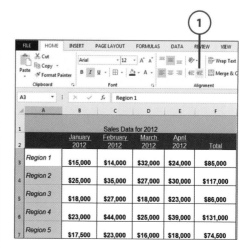

2. To decrease the indent, select the cell or range whose indent you want to decrease.

3. Click the Decrease Indent command to decrease the number of indents.

4. The indentation is decreased.

Increasing Column Width

To make the effect of the indentation stand out, you might need to increase the width of the indented column. To do so, refer to the task "Changing Column Width" earlier in this part.

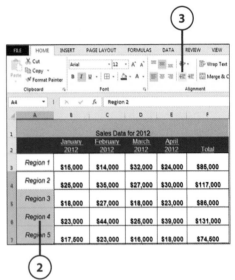

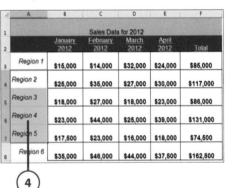

Clearing Formatting

Excel enables you to quickly clear all the formatting you have added to cell data, returning numbers and text to their original format.

1. Select the cells whose formatting you want to clear.

2. On the Home tab, click the down arrow next to the Clear command, and then choose Clear Formats.

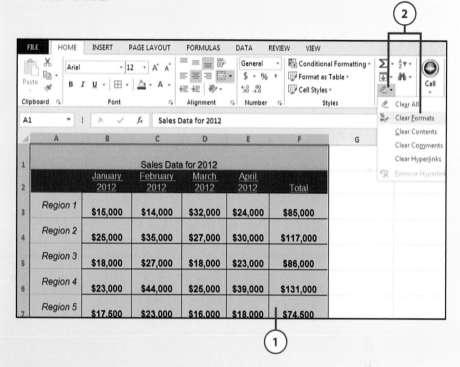

3. The cell data remains, but all the formatting is gone.

More Clear Options

If you choose Clear Contents, the formatting remains intact, but the text and data (contents) are deleted (just as if you simply pressed the Delete key on the keyboard). If you choose Clear All, all the formatting and contents (and comments) are removed from the cell.

Hiding and Unhiding Rows

Hiding rows is a good way to hide calculations that aren't critical for your audience to see. You also can hide other rows that you want to include in the worksheet but don't want to display. It's tricky to unhide a row because you need a way to select the hidden row. This task shows you how.

1. Click any cell in the row, or click the whole row that you want to hide.

2. Click the drop-down arrow next to the Format command on the Home tab.

3. Select Hide & Unhide and then click Hide Rows.

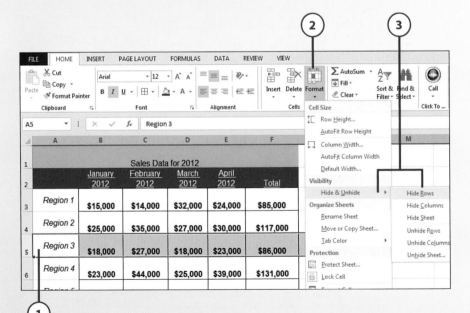

4. You can tell when a row is hidden by the nonsequential jump in the row numbers. For instance, if row 5 is hidden, you see rows 3, 4, 6, 7, and so on.

	A	B	C	D	E	F
1			Sales Data for 2012			
2		January 2012	February 2012	March 2012	April 2012	Total
3	Region 1	$15,000	$14,000	$32,000	$24,000	$85,000
4	Region 2	$25,000	$35,000	$27,000	$30,000	$117,000
6	Region 4	$23,000	$44,000	$25,000	$39,000	$131,000
7	Region 5	$17,500	$23,000	$16,000	$18,000	$74,500
8	Region 6	$35,000	$46,000	$44,000	$37,500	$162,500

5. To unhide the row, select the rows above and below the hidden row.

6. Click the drop-down arrow next to the Format command on the Home tab.

7. Select Hide & Unhide and then click Unhide Rows.

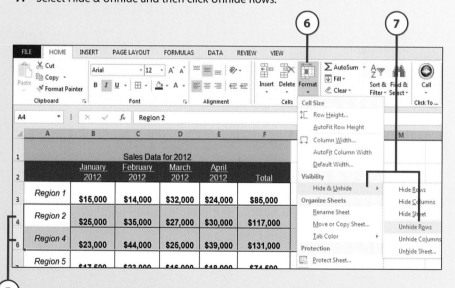

Printing Hidden Elements

Hidden elements, whether they're rows, columns, or worksheets, don't print when you print the worksheet.

Dragging to Hide Rows

Every row has a top border and bottom border (the lines that separate the row numbers). You can click and drag any row's bottom border to either make the row taller or shorter depending on which direction you drag it (up or down). If you drag the bottom border of a row so that it is touching its top border, you can see that the row is effectively hidden. That is to say, you can drag the bottom border of a row so that it is practically zero height.

Hiding and Unhiding Columns

Hiding columns is a good way to hide calculations that aren't critical for your audience to see. You also can hide columns that you want to include in the worksheet but don't want to display. It's tricky to unhide a column because you need a way of selecting the hidden column. This task shows you how.

1. Click any cell in the column, or click the whole column that you want to hide.

2. Click the drop-down arrow next to the Format command on the Home tab.

3. Select Hide & Unhide and then click Hide Columns.

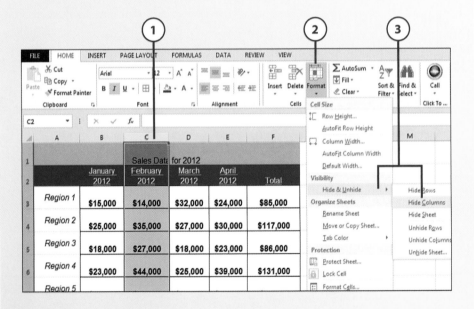

4. You can tell when a column is hidden by the nonsequential jump in the column letters. For example, if column C is hidden, you see columns A, B, D, and so on.

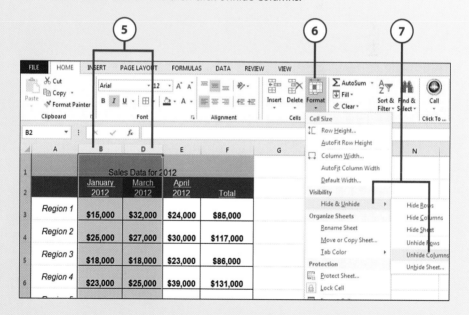

	A	B	D	E	F
1		Sales Data for 2012			
2		January 2012	March 2012	April 2012	Total
3	Region 1	$15,000	$32,000	$24,000	$85,000
4	Region 2	$25,000	$27,000	$30,000	$117,000
5	Region 3	$18,000	$18,000	$23,000	$86,000
6	Region 4	$23,000	$25,000	$39,000	$131,000
7	Region 5	$17,500	$16,000	$18,000	$74,500

5. To unhide the column, select the columns to the left and right of the hidden column.

6. Click the drop-down arrow next to the Format command on the Home tab.

7. Select Hide & Unhide and then click Unhide Columns.

Dragging to Hide Columns

Every column has a left border and right border (the lines that separate the column letters). You can click and drag any column's right border to either make the column wider or more narrow depending on which direction you drag it (left or right). If you drag the right border of a column so that it touches its left border, you can see that the column is effectively hidden. That is to say, you can drag the right border of a column so that it is practically zero width.

Hiding and Unhiding a Worksheet

Often, you might have worksheets that are meant for your eyes only. An example of this would be a worksheet where you document changes in the workbook over the course of development. This kind of worksheet would be administrative in nature and not meant for your audience. In this scenario, hiding the worksheet would be ideal.

1. After you select the tab of any sheet you want to hide, right-click the tab and choose Hide. Excel hides the sheet.

2. To unhide the sheet, right-click any tab and choose Unhide.

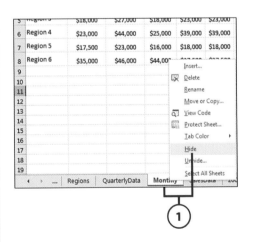

3. The Unhide dialog box opens, listing sheets that are hidden in your workbook. Click the worksheet name you want to unhide.

4. Click the Ok button.

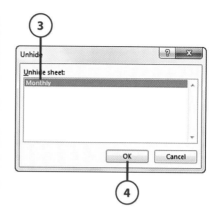

A Hidden Sheet Is Not a Protected Sheet

Be aware that savvy users will know how to look for and unhide your hidden sheets. Do not count on hidden sheets to reliably protect sensitive information. For data protection, consider password protecting your workbook as shown in Chapter 2.

Using Format as Table

Using all the formatting capabilities discussed to this point, you could format your worksheets in an effective and professional manner—but it might take a while to get good at it. In the meantime, you can use Excel's Format as Table feature, which can format selected cells using predefined formats. This feature is a quick way to format large amounts of data and provides ideas on how to manually format data.

1. Select the cells to which you want to apply Format as Table.

2. Click on the down-arrow next to the Format as Table command (found on the Home tab); then scroll through the available formats, and click the one you want to apply to your data.

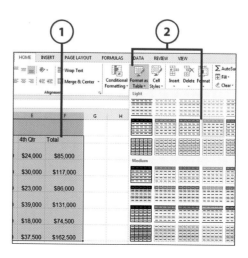

3. Click OK on the next pop-up to confirm that the selected range is correct.

4. The AutoFormat is applied.

Modifying Format As Table

If you go to the Design tab and then run your cursor over the different styles in the Table Styles group, the selected ranges change accordingly so that you can see a preview of what that style does to the data.

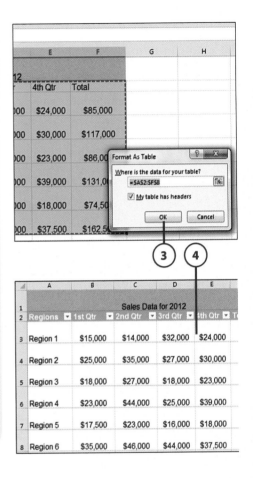

Copying Formatting

If you have formatted a specific cell as you want, you might decide to apply those same formatting options to other cells. Instead of repeating each step in the format process over and over again, you can simply use the Format Painter command.

1. Click the cell with the formatting that you want to copy and apply to other cells.

2. Click the Format Painter command on the Home tab; the mouse pointer changes to a Format Painter pointer (paint-brush symbol).

3. Click and drag the mouse pointer to select the cells to which you want to apply the copied formatting.

4. Release the mouse button. The formatting is applied to the data in the selected cells.

Make Format Painter Persist

Double-click the Format Painter command (instead of single-clicking) and the Format Painter remains active, enabling you to format multiple areas without the need to constantly reactivate it. To turn Format Painter off, simply click it again, or press the Esc button on the keyboard.

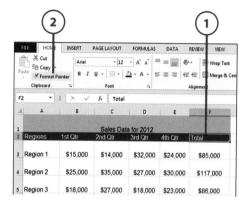
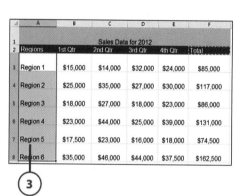
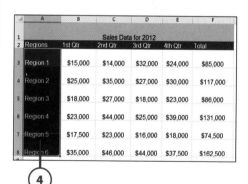

Creating and Applying a Formatting Style

Instead of assigning your data an existing Excel style (for example, Normal, Currency, Percent, and so forth), you can create your own style and apply it to cells. Begin by applying the specific formatting (for example, font, font style, font size, font color, and cell color) that you want the style to have, and then give the style a specific name.

1. Apply any specific cell formatting that you want the style to use in your worksheet (here, Arial, Bold, 12 pt, White text, and Red fill color).

2. With the cell that contains the wanted formatting selected, click the down arrow next to the Cell Styles command on the Home tab. Here, you can see Excel's Cell Styles gallery with all the default styles. Go to the bottom and choose New Cell Style.

3. Type a descriptive name for the new style in the Style name field (for example, Sales Header) and click OK. Your new style displays with the default styles in the Cell Styles gallery.

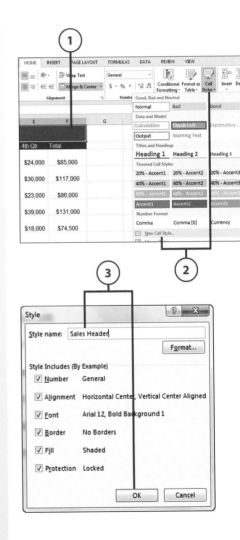

Saving the Style

The next time you exit Excel, you are notified that you made a change to your global template and are asked if you want to save the changes. If you want to keep the style you just created, click the Yes button; otherwise, click the No button.

4. Select the cells to which you want to apply your newly created style.

5. Click the down arrow next to the Cell Styles command on the Home tab, and then choose your custom style in the Custom style group at the top.

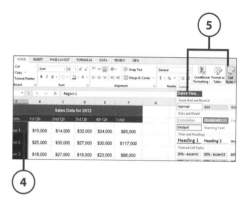

6. The style is applied to the cells you selected.

Default Styles

There are also default styles for Data and Model, Titles and Headings, Themed Cell Styles, and Number Format. You can run your cursor over each option to see how it changes your data prior to selecting it.

	A	B	C	D	E	F
1			Sales Data for 2012			
2	Regions	1st Qtr	2nd Qtr	3rd Qtr	4th Qtr	Total
3	Region 1	$15,000	$14,000	$32,000	$24,000	$85,000
4	Region 2	$25,000	$35,000	$27,000	$30,000	$117,000
5	Region 3	$18,000	$27,000	$18,000	$23,000	$86,000
6	Region 4	$23,000	$44,000	$25,000	$39,000	$131,000
7	Region 5	$17,500	$23,000	$16,000	$18,000	$74,500
8	Region 6	$35,000	$46,000	$44,000	$37,500	$162,500

Using Conditional Formatting

There might be times when you want the formatting of a cell to depend on the value it contains. For this, use conditional formatting, which enables you to specify conditions that, when met, cause the cell to be formatted in the manner defined for that condition. If none of the conditions are met, the cell keeps its original formatting. For example, you can set a conditional format such that if sales for a particular month are greater than $30,000, the data in the cell is bold and red.

1. Select the cells to which you want to apply conditional formatting; then click the down arrow next to the Conditional Formatting command on the Home tab, and choose New Rule.

2. In the New Formatting Rule dialog box, choose the Format Only Cells That Contain option.

3. Leave the first drop-down list as Cell Value. Open the second drop-down list to select the type of condition (for example, Greater Than).

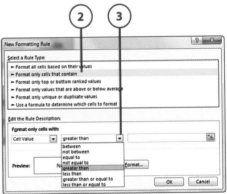

Painting a Format onto Other Cells

You can copy the conditional formatting from one cell to another. To do so, click the cell whose formatting you want to copy; then click the Format Painter command. Finally, drag over the cells to which you want to copy the formatting.

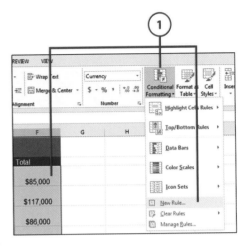

4. Type the value of the condition (the number that the cells must be "greater than").

5. Click the Format command to set the format to use when the condition is met.

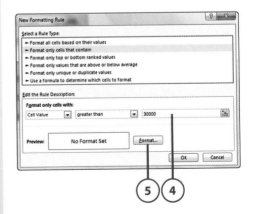

6. Click the options you want to set in the Format Cells dialog box (for example, Red in the Color field and Bold in the Font style list), and click OK.

7. Click OK in the Format Cells dialog box.

8. Excel applies the formatting to any cells that meet the condition you specified.

When to Use Conditional Formatting

Use conditional formatting to draw attention to values that have different meanings, depending on whether they are positive or negative, such as profit and loss values.

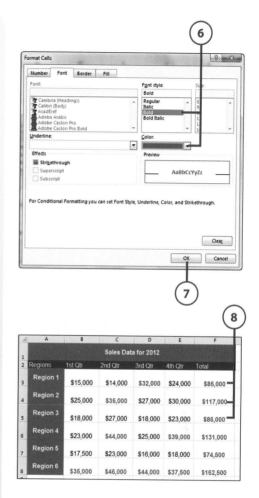

Formula bar

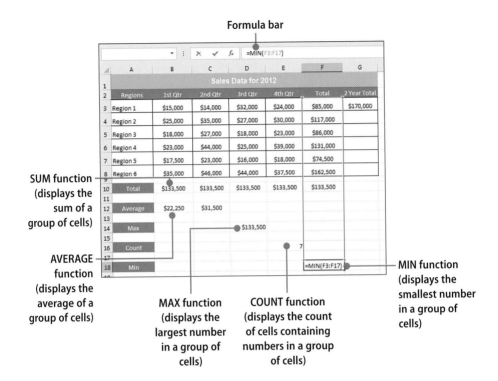

SUM function (displays the sum of a group of cells)

AVERAGE function (displays the average of a group of cells)

MAX function (displays the largest number in a group of cells)

COUNT function (displays the count of cells containing numbers in a group of cells)

MIN function (displays the smallest number in a group of cells)

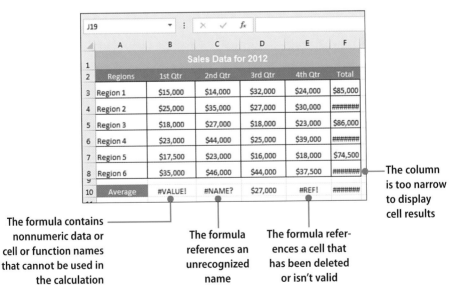

The formula contains nonnumeric data or cell or function names that cannot be used in the calculation

The formula references an unrecognized name

The formula references a cell that has been deleted or isn't valid

The column is too narrow to display cell results

This chapter walks you through the ins and outs of using Excel formulas and functions. By the end of this chapter, you will be well equipped to start building your own formulas!

→ Using AutoSum calculations

→ Entering and editing a formula

→ Copying a formula

→ Assigning names to a cell or range

→ Working with functions

→ Using Auto-Calculate

→ Recognizing and fixing errors

→ Checking for formula references (PRECEDENTS)

→ Checking for cell references (DEPENDENTS)

5

Working with Formulas and Functions

A *formula* is essentially a series of instructions you give Excel to return a value. These instructions can be mathematical operations, or a call to a built-in Excel function. Excel typically displays the result of a formula in a cell as either numeric or textual data.

Functions are abbreviated formulas that perform specific operations on a group of values. Excel provides more than 250 functions that can help you with tasks ranging from determining loan payments to calculating investment returns. For example, the SUM function automatically adds up the numeric values within a given range.

Using AutoSum Calculations

Excel has several built-in formulas that perform the most commonly used calculations for you. These built-in calculations include Sum, Average, Count, Max, and Min. You start your exploration of Excel formulas and functions with these predefined calculations. The most prominent of these is the AutoSum or sum. You'll probably use the AutoSum formula a lot—it adds numbers in a range of cells.

1. Click in the cell in which you want the result of the AutoSum operation to appear, which is called the *resultant cell*.

2. Click the AutoSum command on the Home tab.

3. Excel selects the most obvious range of numbers and puts a dotted line around the cells. Press Enter to accept the range, or use the mouse to select alternative cells.

4. Click the resultant cell to make it the active cell. The formula displays on the Formula bar.

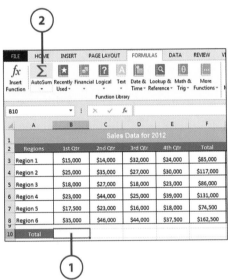

___

AutoSum Shortcut Key

Excel provides an easy way to implement the AutoSum via a shortcut key. Simply go to your keyboard and enter the combination of Alt and the equal sign (=). Excel performs the AutoSum for you. At that point, just press Enter on your keyboard to accept the AutoSum calculation.

___

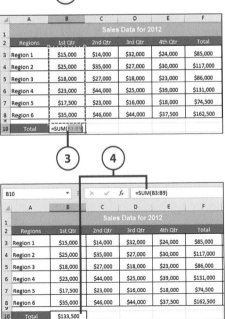

Find a Cell Average (AVERAGE)

You can use Excel's AVERAGE function to determine the average of each quarter per region.

1. Click the cell in which you want the result of the AVERAGE function to appear, which is called the *resultant cell*.

2. Click the down arrow next to the AutoSum command on the Home tab, and choose Average from the list that appears.

3. Excel selects the most obvious range of numbers and puts a dotted line around the cells. Press Enter to accept the range, or use the mouse to select alternative cells.

4. Click the resultant cell to make it the active cell. The formula displays on the Formula bar.

Selecting Specific Cells for Your Calculation

If you don't want to use the range of cells that Excel selects for you, click the first cell you want, hold down the Ctrl key, and click each additional cell you would like to include in the calculation. When you finish selecting the cells you want to calculate, press Enter to see the result. Alternatively, if you let Excel select the cells for you but Excel doesn't select exactly the right set of cells, you can resize the selection by clicking the first cell to include, holding down the Shift key, and clicking the last cell to include.

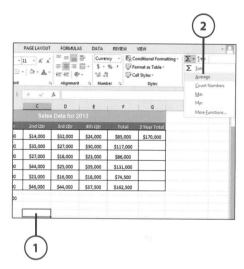

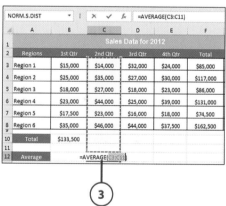

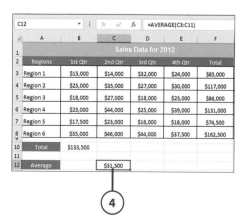

Find the Largest Cell Amount (MAX)

As its name suggests, the MAX function returns the largest/maximum number in any given range. You typically use this function if you need to dynamically reference the largest number in other formulas. For example, you can use Excel's MAX function to determine the quarter in which you had the most sales. Although it's easy to see this information with your eyes, the Quarter with the most sales changes as each quarter passes. Instead of manually keeping up with which quarter is the king of sales, the MAX function does that for you.

1. Click the cell in which you want the result of the MAX function to appear, which is called the *resultant cell*.

2. Click the down arrow next to the AutoSum command on the Home tab, and choose Max from the list that appears.

3. Excel selects the most obvious range of numbers and puts a dotted line around the cells. Press Enter to accept the range or use the mouse to select alternative cells.

4. Click the resultant cell to make it the active cell. The formula displays on the Formula bar.

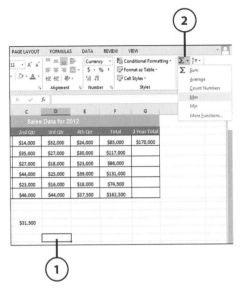

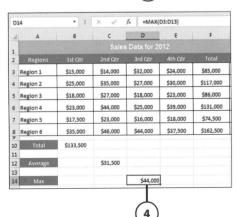

Find the Smallest Cell Amount (MIN)

As its name suggests, the MIN function returns the smallest/minimum number in any given range. This is the direct opposite of the MAX function, which returns the largest number in a range. You would typically use Excel's MIN function to determine the lowest performing Region, or Market, or whatever else you want to measure. This quickly gives you a reference point for the lowest number in your data.

1. Click the cell in which you want the result of the function to appear, which is called the *resultant cell*.

2. Click the down arrow next to the AutoSum command on the Home tab, and choose Min from the list that appears.

3. Excel selects the most obvious range of numbers and puts a dotted line around the cells. Press Enter to accept the range, or use the mouse to select alternative cells.

4. Click the resultant cell to make it the active cell. The formula displays on the Formula bar.

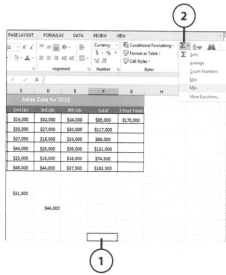

	A	B	C	D	E	F
1			Sales Data for 2012			
2	Regions	1st Qtr	2nd Qtr	3rd Qtr	4th Qtr	Total
3	Region 1	$15,000	$14,000	$32,000	$24,000	$85,000
4	Region 2	$25,000	$35,000	$27,000	$30,000	$117,000
5	Region 3	$18,000	$27,000	$18,000	$23,000	$86,000
6	Region 4	$23,000	$44,000	$25,000	$39,000	$131,000
7	Region 5	$17,500	$23,000	$16,000	$18,000	$74,500
8	Region 6	$35,000	$46,000	$44,000	$37,500	$162,500
10	Total	$133,500				
11						
12	Average		$31,500			
13						
14	Max			$44,000		
15						
16	Count					
17						
18	Min					=MIN(F3:F17)

	A	B	C	D	E	F
1			Sales Data for 2012			
2	Regions	1st Qtr	2nd Qtr	3rd Qtr	4th Qtr	Total
3	Region 1	$15,000	$14,000	$32,000	$24,000	$85,000
4	Region 2	$25,000	$35,000	$27,000	$30,000	$117,000
5	Region 3	$18,000	$27,000	$18,000	$23,000	$86,000
6	Region 4	$23,000	$44,000	$25,000	$39,000	$131,000
7	Region 5	$17,500	$23,000	$16,000	$18,000	$74,500
8	Region 6	$35,000	$46,000	$44,000	$37,500	$162,500
10	Total	$133,500				
11						
12	Average		$31,500			
13						
14	Max			$44,000		
15						
16	Count					
17						
18	Min					$74,500

Count the Number of Cells (COUNT)

As you might have guessed, the COUNT function literally counts the number of data points in any given range. Suppose you want to know how many values (data points) are in your data table; you can use Excel's COUNT function to count the number of cells in a selected range.

1. Click the cell in which you want the result of the COUNT function to appear, which is called the *resultant cell*.

2. Click the down arrow next to the AutoSum command on the Home tab, and choose Count Numbers from the list that appears.

3. Excel selects the most obvious range of numbers and puts a dotted line around the cells. Press Enter to accept the range or use the mouse to select alternative cells.

4. Click the resultant cell to make it the active cell. The formula displays on the Formula bar.

Counting Text Values

The COUNT function works only if the range you count is numbers-based. That is, it counts only numeric values (not text). To count the data points in a range that contains text, you can use the COUNTA function. Using the COUNTA function counts both numeric and textual values. To use COUNTA, simply edit your formula by replacing the word COUNT with COUNTA.

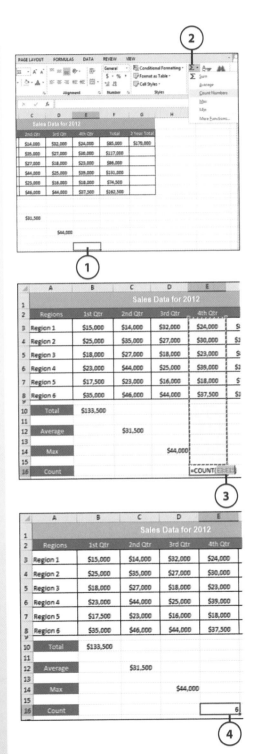

Entering a Formula

Another way to use a formula is to type it directly into the cell. You can include any cells in your formula; they do not need to be next to each other. Also, you can combine mathematic operations—for example, C3+C4–D5.

1. Click the cell in which you want the result of the formula to appear, which is called the *resultant cell*.

2. Type = (the equal sign) followed by the references of the cells containing the data you want to total (for example, F3+F4+F5+F6+F7+F8). Press Enter.

3. Click the resultant cell to make it the active cell; the values in the specified cells are added together.

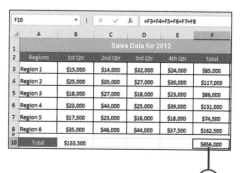

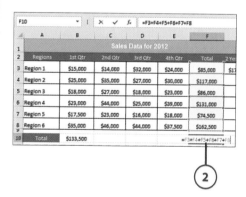

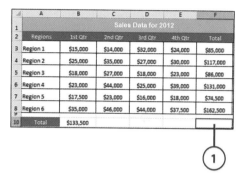

ORDER OF OPERATION

You must remember that Excel evaluates and performs all calculations based on the standard mathematical Order of Operations. The basic order of operations follows:

Calculations within parentheses are performed first. Then multiplication and division operations are performed from left to right. Finally, addition and subtraction operations are performed from left to right.

So consider this example. The correct answer to (2+3)*4 is 20. However, if you leave off the parentheses, as in 2+3*4, Excel performs the calculation like this: 3*4 = 12 + 2 = 14. The order of operator precedence mandates that Excel perform multiplication before subtraction. Entering 2+3*4 gives you the wrong answer. Because Excel evaluates and performs all calculations in parentheses first, placing 2+3 inside parentheses ensures the correct answer.

Editing a Formula or Function

After you enter a formula or function, you can change the values in the referenced cells, and Excel automatically recalculates the result based on the changes. You can include any cells in a formula or function; they do not need to be next to each other.

1. Click the cell you want to edit; the function displays on the Formula bar.

2. Click the Insert Function command on the Formula bar to open the Function Arguments dialog box. (If using a formula, the Insert Function dialog box displays.)

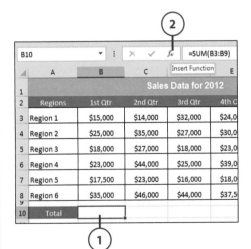

3. Type the changes to your function. For example, change the cells being calculated to B3–B8 instead of B3–B9. Click OK.

4. The changes are made and the result appears in the cell.

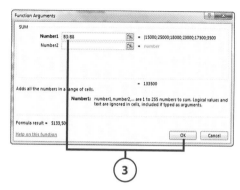

Pressing F2

Instead of using the Function Arguments dialog box to edit your formulas, you can press the F2 key and edit your formula just like you would for regular text or data on the Formula bar.

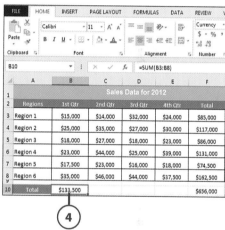

Copying a Formula

When you build your worksheet, you might want to use the same data and formulas in more than one cell. With Excel's Copy command, you can create the initial data or formula once and then place copies in the appropriate cells. For example, suppose you want to find the average sales per quarter in other sales regions. To do so, create the formula for the first region and then copy it to cells for the other regions. Excel automatically figures out how to change the cell ranges to which the formula should apply.

1. Click the cell that contains the function you want to copy.

2. Click the Copy command on the Home tab; a line surrounds the cell you are copying.

3. Click the cell or cells into which you want to paste the formula.

4. Press Enter (or Ctrl+V) to paste the formula into each of the selected cells.

Increasing Cell Width

If you paste a copied formula, you might need to alter the size of your columns to accommodate the new size of the data in the cell. To automatically make an entire column (or multiple columns) fit the width of the widest cell in that column (or columns), move the cursor over the right side of the column header, and double-click when the cursor changes to a two-headed arrow.

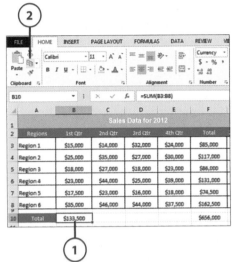

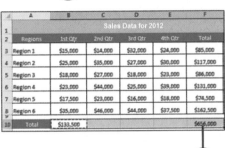

Assigning Names to a Cell or Range

You can create range names that make it easier to create formulas and move to that range. For example, a formula that refers to a range named 1stQtr is easier to understand than one named B4:B9. Not only is it easier to remember a name than the cell addresses, but Excel also displays the range name in the Name box—next to the Formula bar. You can name a single cell or a selected range in the worksheet.

1. Select the cell or range you want to name.

2. Click in the Name box; type the wanted range name and press Enter.

3. Highlight the range and note that the name appears in the Name box.

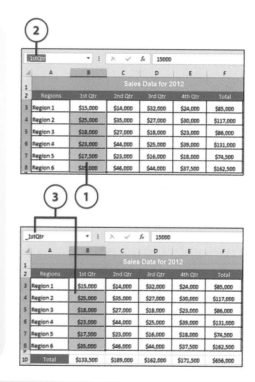

RULES FOR NAMING RANGES

Excel has a few basic rules for the naming of ranges. First, you must start your range names with a letter or an underscore. That is to say, you cannot start your range names with numbers. You can, however, use numbers anywhere else in your range names. Second, you can include uppercase and lowercase letters, but you cannot use spaces. Third, you can use up to 255 characters, but as a best practice, you should always strive to keep your range names short and pithy. Finally, you cannot use a name that conflicts with a built-in range or cell reference. For example, you can't use A1 as a range name.

Referencing Names in a Function

One of the reasons you create a name for a cell or group of cells is so that you can easily refer to that cell or range in a function. That way, rather than typing or selecting a range or cell, you can type the name or select it from the Paste Name dialog box.

1. Click in the cell in which you want the result of the formula to appear, which is called the *resultant cell.*

2. Type the function in the cell using a named cell or range—for example, =AVERAGE(_1stQtr). As you type the name, you should see a list of named ranges pop up below the cell.

3. Click a named range to select it.

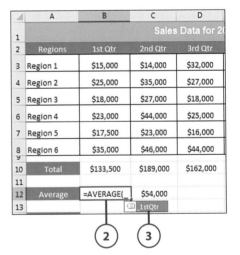

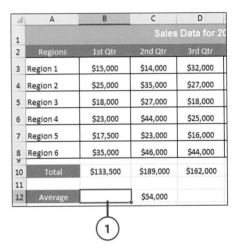

4. Press Enter and Excel displays the result of the formula.

◢	A	B	C	D
1				Sales Data for 2(
2	Regions	1st Qtr	2nd Qtr	3rd Qtr
3	Region 1	$15,000	$14,000	$32,000
4	Region 2	$25,000	$35,000	$27,000
5	Region 3	$18,000	$27,000	$18,000
6	Region 4	$23,000	$44,000	$25,000
7	Region 5	$17,500	$23,000	$16,000
8	Region 6	$35,000	$46,000	$44,000
9				
10	Total	$133,500	$189,000	$162,000
11				
12	Average	$22,250	$54,000	

④

Quickly Retrieve a Range Name

If you forget the name of a range while you are typing a formula, go to the Formula tab, and click the Use in Formula drop-down. You see a list of the available range names. Simply choose the one you want to use. The range name is automatically placed in the formula.

Deleting a Range Name

To delete a range name, go to the Formulas tab and click the Name Manager. Click the range name you want to get rid of and then click the Delete command. Click OK to confirm the deletion.

Using Functions Across Worksheets

You can use cell references from other worksheets in your calculations. For example, suppose you have two worksheets that contain the calculations for the total sales by region for a particular year. In a third worksheet, you want to calculate the total sales by region for the last 2 years. You can reference the cells in the first two worksheets that contain the totals and perform calculations on them in the third worksheet.

1. Click in the cell in which you want the result of the formula to appear, which is called the *resultant cell*.

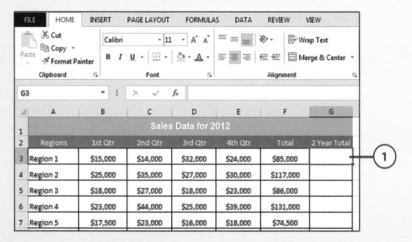

2. This example adds the total for the current year (2012) to last year's data in another worksheet (2011), so you start the formula by referencing the 2012 total; then you enter a + (plus sign).

3. Click the tab of the worksheet that contains the cell you want to reference in the calculation.

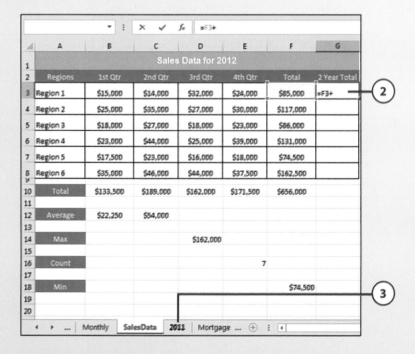

Using Worksheet Name References

Instead of switching back and forth between worksheets, you can manually type the reference to the worksheet name directly in your formulas. Simply use the location of the cell in a particular worksheet (column letter and row number) in addition to the sheet name—for example, Sheet1!A1. If your sheet name contains spaces, you need to enclose your sheet name with single quotes— for example, 'My Second Sheet'!A1.

4. Click the cell that you want to use in your calculation; it appears next to the worksheet name on the Formula bar.

5. Press Enter. Excel performs the calculation and returns you to the original worksheet.

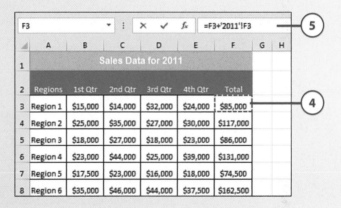

6. Click the resultant cell to make it the active cell. The function displays on the Formula bar.

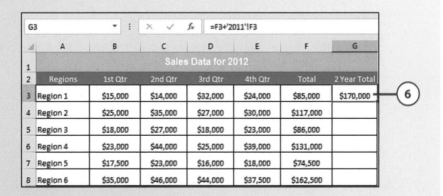

Be Aware of Worksheet Name References

Each cell you reference from another worksheet must be prefaced with its worksheet name. For example, if you have the formula =SUM(Sheet1!A1+B1) in cell C3 of Sheet2, it references cell A1 from Sheet1 and B1 from Sheet2. If you need to reference both A1 and B1 from Sheet 1, you must include the worksheet name with both cell references, like so: =SUM(Sheet1!A1+Sheet1!B1).

Using Auto-Calculate

Suppose you want to see a function performed on some of your data—in this example, to determine the lowest quarterly sales goal of any region in 2012—but you don't want to add the function directly into the worksheet. Excel's Auto-Calculate feature can help.

1. Select the cells that you want to Auto-Calculate.

2. The Status Bar now shows you the Average, Count, and Sum.

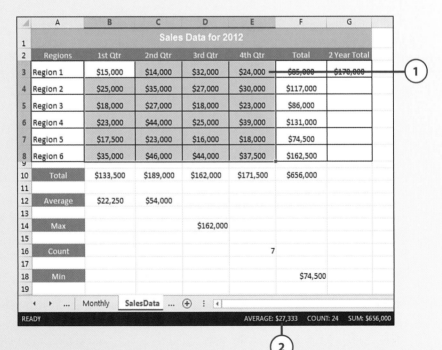

3. Right-click the Status Bar and click each option you want to enable or disable.

4. Observe your new Auto Calculation(s).

Turning Off Auto-Calculate

You can turn off the Auto-Calculate feature by right-clicking the Status Bar and unselecting each option that is selected.

Finding and Using Excel Functions

In the old days, you needed to know the name of the Excel function you wanted to use. Now, however, Excel makes it easy to find the function you need—all you need to know is what you want the function to do. In the next few tasks, you walk through the creation of several functions using the Insert Function command.

1. Click the Insert Function (fx) command next to the Formula bar.

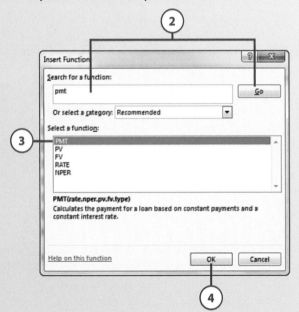

2. Type a description of the function you are looking for in the Search for a Function text box, and press Enter. (Or click the Go button.)

3. Scroll through the list in the Select a Function box and select a function to read a description of it.

4. Click OK after you find the function you want.

5. Excel walks you through the process of entering the function's arguments in the Function Arguments dialog box. Click OK when you finish entering its arguments.

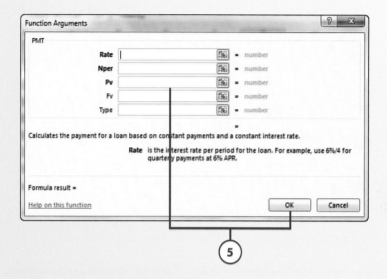

Function Arguments Help

If you need help entering your function arguments, click the Help on This Function link in the bottom-left corner of the Function Arguments dialog box.

Calculate a Loan Payment (PMT)

Using Excel, you can determine a monthly loan payment based on a constant interest rate, a specific number of pay periods, and the current loan amount.

1. Click in the cell in which you want the result of the function to appear, which is called the *resultant cell*.

2. Click the Insert Function (fx) command next to the Formula bar.

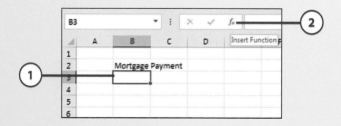

3. The Insert Function dialog box opens. Click the down arrow next to the Or Select a Category field, and choose Financial from the list that appears.

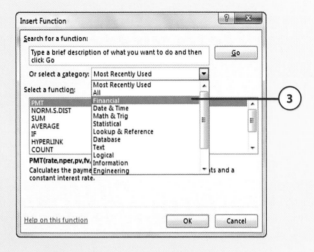

4. A list of financial-related functions appears in the Select a Function list. Scroll through the list to locate the PMT function and double-click it.

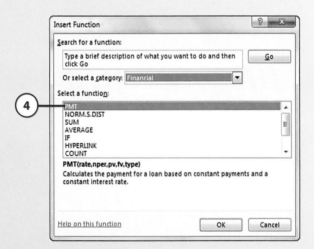

Function Arguments Help

If you need help while you are entering your function arguments, click the Help on This Function link in the bottom-left corner of the Function Arguments dialog box.

Negative Payment

Your resulting payment is a negative number because payments are considered a debit.

5. In the Rate field, type the interest rate per period. For example, type 6%/12 for monthly payments on a 6 percent annual percentage rate (APR).

6. In the Nper field, type the total number of loan payments. For example, type 360 if you'll be making 12 payments per year on a 30-year loan.

7. In the Pv field, type the present value of the loan—for example, 150000.

8. Click OK.

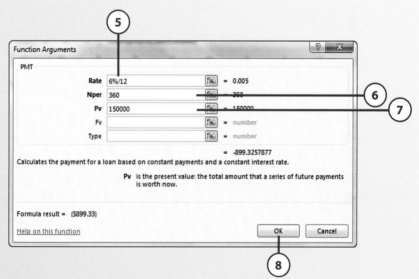

9. Excel calculates the payment and inserts it in the resultant cell.

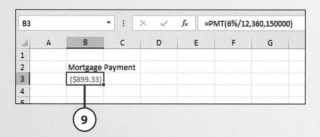

Type Argument

If you don't enter a number in the Type argument, it defaults to 0, which means that the last payment pays off the mortgage loan. (This is because mortgages are paid in arrears—at the end of the payment period). If you are calculating a car payment, you might put a 1 in the Type argument because you make your payments at the beginning of the payment period. A 1 versus a 0 makes a slight difference in the calculation because of the interest accrued.

Perform a Logical Test Function (IF)

Using Excel, you can perform a logical test function—for example, to indicate whether scores equal a passing or failing grade based on an established set of criteria.

1.   Click in the cell in which you want the result of the function to appear, which is called the *resultant cell*.

2.   Click the Insert Function (fx) command next to the Formula bar.

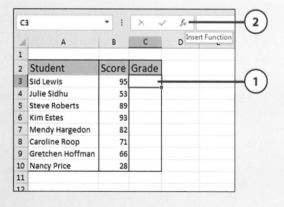

3. The Insert Function dialog box opens. Click the down arrow next to the Or Select a Category field, and choose Logical from the list that appears.

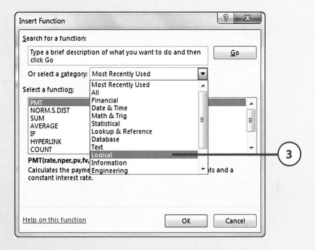

4. A list of logical functions appears in the Select a Function list. Scroll through the list to locate the IF function and double-click it.

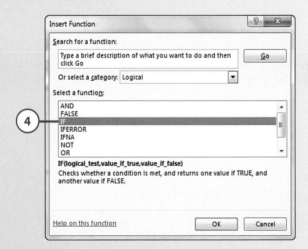

Embedded IFs

You can set up embedded IF statements to use in your logical test. For example, suppose scores between 90–100 are an A, 80–89 are a B, 70–79 are a C, 60–69 are a D, and scores 59 and lower are an F. Your formula might look like this:
=IF(B3>89, "A", IF(B3>79, "B", IF(B3>69, "C", IF(B3>59, "D", "F")).

5. In the Logical_test field, type the condition to determine whether a grade is above 70. The logical test is whether the cell is greater than 70; for example, B3>70.

6. In the Value_if_true field, type the value you want to use if the grade is above 70 (that is, a passing grade)—for example, "Pass".

7. In the Value_if_false field, type the value you want to use if the grade is below 70 (that is, a failing grade)—for example, "Fail".

8. Click OK.

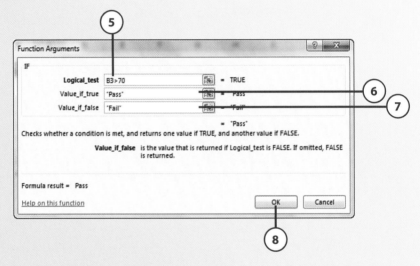

9. Excel performs the logical test and inserts the result in the resultant cell.

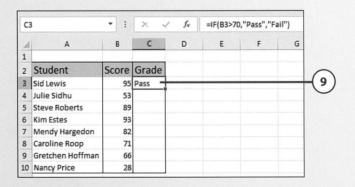

Quick Help with Functions

You can press the F1 key on your keyboard any time you're typing up an Excel function to automatically be brought to that function's help screen.

Conditionally Sum a Range(SUMIF)

Using Excel, you can add the data in a range, given certain criteria. This might be useful if, for instance, you need to total the current monthly sales for all sales reps who match a specific criterion—for example, who are all in the same sales region.

1. Click in the cell in which you want the result of the function to appear, which is called the *resultant cell*.

2. Click the Insert Function (fx) command next to the Formula bar.

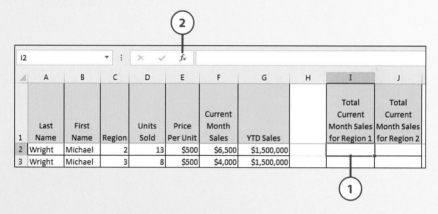

3. The Insert Function dialog box opens. Click the down arrow next to the Or Select a Category field and choose Math & Trig from the list that appears.

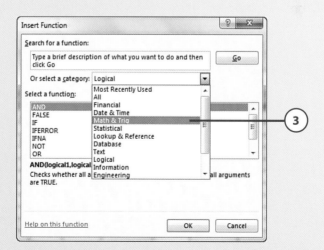

4. A list of math and trig functions appears in the Select a Function list. Scroll through the list to locate the SUMIF function, and double-click it.

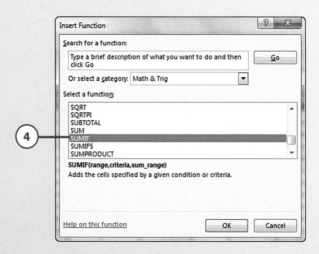

5. In the Range field, type the range of cells whose contents you want to review—for example, C2:C79. (You can also click directly in the worksheet to select the cells.)

6. In the Criteria field, type the criterion you want to check in the range—in this case, type 1 because you want to add sales data from Region 1 only.

7. In the Sum_range field, type the range of cells that match your criterion—in this case, F2:F79, which contains the current month sales data.

8. Click OK.

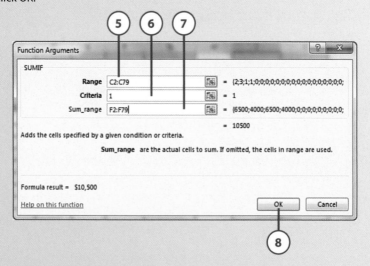

9. Excel adds the range given your criteria and inserts the result in the resultant cell.

| | I2 | | ▾ | ⋮ | × | ✓ | f_x | =SUMIF(C2:C79,1,F2:F79) | | | |

	A	B	C	D	E	F	G	H	I	J
						Current			Total Current	Total Current
1	Last Name	First Name	Region	Units Sold	Price Per Unit	Month Sales	YTD Sales		Month Sales for Region 1	Month Sales for Region 2
2	Wright	Michael	2	13	$500	$6,500	$1,500,000		$10,500	
3	Wright	Michael	3	8	$500	$4,000	$1,500,000			

⑨

Range Selection

In addition to typing specific Range and Sum_range arguments, you can click in the worksheet and select each range of cells using the mouse.

COUNTIF

Instead of totaling cells that meet a criterion with SUMIF, you can use COUNTIF to count the number of cells in a range that meet a specific criterion. For example, instead of totaling your sales data, maybe you want to know how many regional quarters were less than $20,000.

Find the Future Value of an Investment (FV)

If you open a 3 percent interest-bearing money market account with $100 in January and make deposits of $100 each month, how much money will you have at the end of the year? Excel can help you calculate the future value of an amount of money, based on a constant interest rate, over a specific number of periods in which you make a constant payment.

1. Click in the cell in which you want the result of the function to appear, which is called the *resultant cell.*

2. Click the Insert Function (fx) command next to the Formula bar.

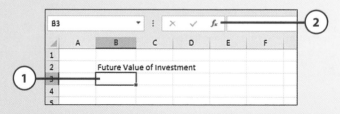

3. The Insert Function dialog box opens. Click the down arrow next to the Or Select a Category field, and choose Financial from the list that appears.

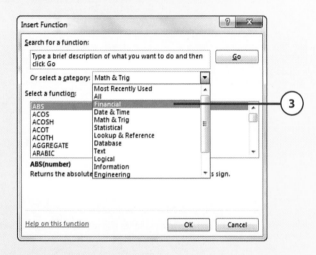

4. A list of financial-related functions appears in the Select a Function list. Scroll through the list to locate the FV function, and double-click it.

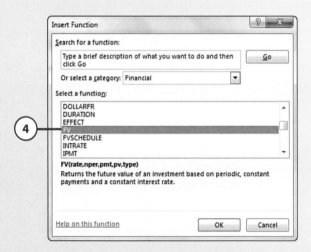

5. In the Rate field, type the interest rate per period. For example, type 3%/12 for monthly accrual on a 3 percent interest-bearing account.

6. In the Nper field, type the total number of payments for the investment (in this example, 12 deposits).

7. In the Pmt field, type the amount to be paid in each deposit—in this case, –100.

8. Click OK.

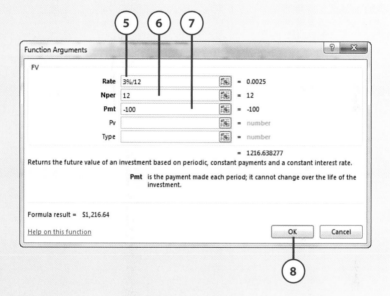

9. Excel calculates the future investment value and inserts it in the resultant cell.

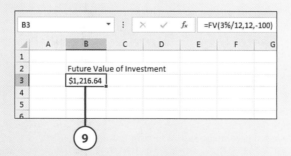

Negative Payments

Because you are making a payment with each deposit, you need to make sure the Pmt argument is a negative value.

Recognizing and Fixing Errors

Excel notifies you when there are errors in your data by displaying different error descriptions in the cell that contains the error. For example, when a cell contains the value ####, it means that the column that contains that value is not wide enough to display the actual data. Simply widen the column to see the cell's contents. The next few tasks explain the various types of errors and how to fix them.

1. If one of the cells in your worksheet contains the #### error, click the cell's column border and drag it to increase the column width.

2. When you let go of the dragged border, the error disappears and the cell's actual data is displayed.

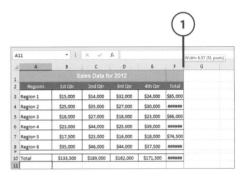

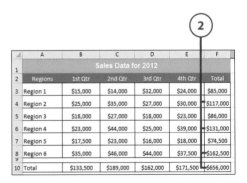

Beginning with Larger Columns

It is a good idea to start out with columns that are larger than you need. Then you can decrease their size while you format the worksheet.

AutoFitting Column Widths

To automatically make an entire column (or multiple columns) fit the width of the widest cell in that column (or columns), move the cursor over the right side of the column header, and double-click when the cursor changes to a two-headed arrow.

Fix the #DIV/0! Error

Excel notifies you when there are errors in your data by displaying different error descriptions in the cell that contains the error. For example, when a cell contains the #DIV/0! error, it means that the formula is trying to divide a number by 0, or by an empty cell.

1. In the cell you want to use as the resultant cell, type a formula to obtain an average. For example, type =SUM(B10/B9) in cell B12, and press Enter.

2. If one of the cells in your worksheet now contains the #DIV/0! error, locate the empty cell referenced by the formula (in this case, cell B9).

3. Click the resultant cell (here, B12), press F2 on the keyboard, and retype the formula to omit the empty cell—in this case, =(B10/B11)—and press Enter.

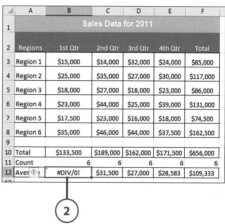

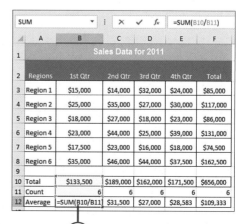

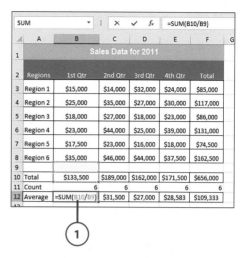

4. The error disappears because it is no longer trying to divide a number by an empty cell.

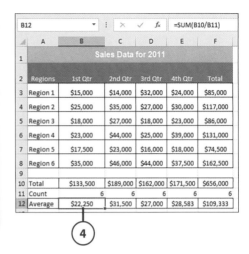

④

Pressing the Delete Key

In this example, you could also press the Delete key in cell B9 to remove the formula.

Fix the #NAME? Error

Excel notifies you when there are errors in your data by displaying different error descriptions in the cell that contains the error. For example, when a cell contains a #NAME? error, it means the formula contains an incorrectly spelled cell or function name.

1. In the cell you want to use as the resultant cell, type the formula you want to use in your calculation. For example, type =CNT(B3:B8) in cell B11, and press Enter.

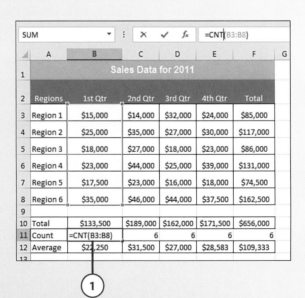

①

2. In this case, you get the #NAME? error because CNT is not the correct spelling for the referenced function. (It is COUNT.)

	A	B	C	D	E	F
1			Sales Data for 2011			
2	Regions	1st Qtr	2nd Qtr	3rd Qtr	4th Qtr	Total
3	Region 1	$15,000	$14,000	$32,000	$24,000	$85,000
4	Region 2	$25,000	$35,000	$27,000	$30,000	$117,000
5	Region 3	$18,000	$27,000	$18,000	$23,000	$86,000
6	Region 4	$23,000	$44,000	$25,000	$39,000	$131,000
7	Region 5	$17,500	$23,000	$16,000	$18,000	$74,500
8	Region 6	$35,000	$46,000	$44,000	$37,500	$162,500
9						
10	Total	$133,500	$189,000	$162,000	$171,500	$656,000
11	Coun	#NAME?	6	6	6	6
12	Average	#NAME?	$31,500	$27,000	$28,583	$109,333

(2)

3. Click the resultant cell (here, B11), press F2 on the keyboard, and retype the formula—in this case, =COUNT(B3:B8)—and press Enter.

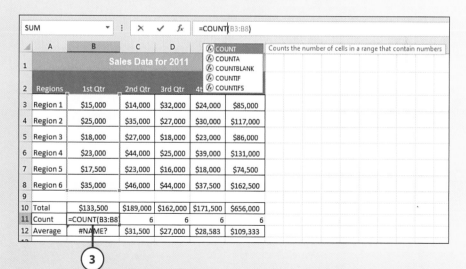

(3)

4. The error disappears because the function is spelled correctly.

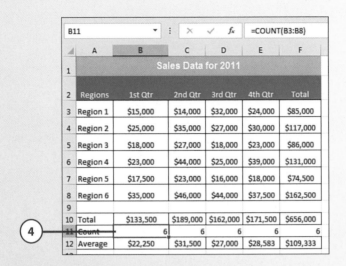

Leveraging the Insert Function Dialog Box

If you are unsure about the exact syntax Excel requires for a function, consider using the Insert Function dialog box (covered earlier in this chapter in the "Finding and Using Excel Functions" section).

Fix the #VALUE! Error

Excel notifies you when there are errors in your data by displaying different error descriptions in the cell that contains the error. For example, when a cell contains a #VALUE? error, it means the formula contains nonnumeric data or cell or function names that cannot be used in the calculation.

1. In the cell you want to use as the resultant cell, type the formula you want to use in your calculation. For example, type =SUM(B2+B4+B5+B6+B7+B8) in cell B10, and press Enter.

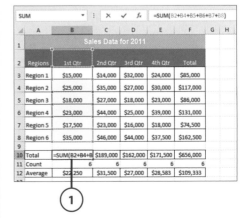

2. In this case, you get the #VALUE! error because the value in cell B2 is textual, not numeric. You won't get the error if you either remove B2 or you replace the formula with =SUM(B2:B8) instead of the plus signs.

3. Click the resultant cell (here, B10), press F2 on the keyboard, and retype the formula—in this case, =SUM(B3+B4+B5+B6+B7+B8)— and press Enter.

4. The error disappears because all cells are now numeric.

Overwriting Cells

See the task "Overwriting and Deleting Data" in Chapter 3, "Entering and Managing Data," to make sure you are correctly overwriting data in cells.

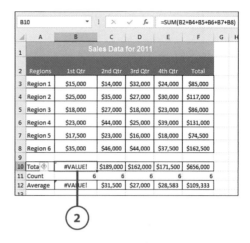

Recognize the #REF! Error

Excel notifies you when there are errors in your data by displaying different error descriptions in the cell that contains the error. For example, when a cell contains a #REF! error, it means the formula contains a reference to a cell that isn't valid. Frequently, this means you deleted a referenced cell. The best solution is to undo your action and review the cells involved in the formula.

1.   In the cell you want to use as the resultant cell, type the formula you want to use in your calculation. For example, type =SUM(B2+C2+D2+E2) and press Enter.

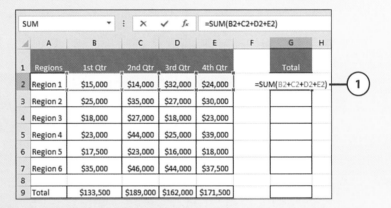

2.   Right-click one of the columns that contains a cell referenced in the formula you just typed (here, column D), and choose Delete from the shortcut menu that appears.

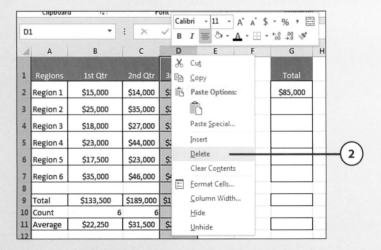

3. In this case, the #REF! error appears because the values in cells referenced in column D are no longer available in the formula.

4. Click the Undo command to correct it.

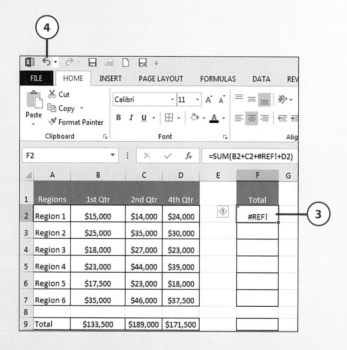

5. The error disappears because the formula values are restored.

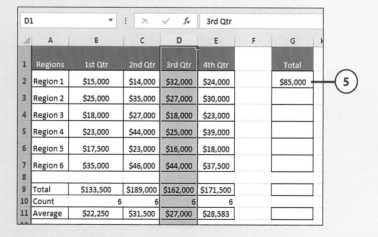

Checking References

If after you undo what caused the #REF! error you want to find out what caused it, see the tasks "Checking for Formula References (Precedents)" and "Checking for Cell References (Dependents)" later in this chapter for more information on checking formula and cell references.

Recognizing Circular References

Excel notifies you when there are errors in your data by displaying different error descriptions in the cell that contains the error. For example, you receive a circular reference error message when one of the cells you are referencing in your calculation is the cell in which you want the calculation to appear.

1. Type the formula you want to use in your calculation. For example, type =SUM(B2+C2+D2+E2+G2) and press Enter.

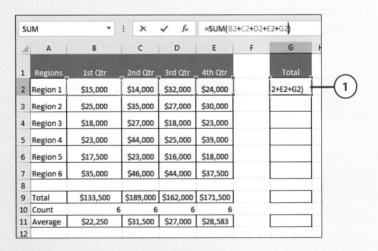

2. Excel displays an error message, notifying you that the formula contains a circular reference. Click OK.

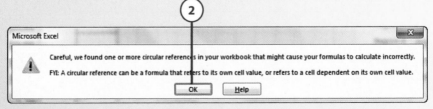

3. Click the resultant cell, press F2 on the keyboard, and edit your formula—in this case, =SUM(B2+C2+D2+E2)—and press Enter.

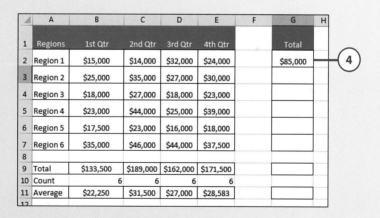

4. The error is fixed because the result cell no longer is in the calculation.

Circular Reference Dialog

If you didn't intend to create a circular reference and you chose OK in the message box, the Circular Reference dialog and Help display to assist you in correcting your actions.

Checking for Formula References (PRECEDENTS)

One way to check a formula to see whether it is referencing the correct cells is to select that formula and then trace all cells referenced in that formula. Cells referenced are called *precedents*.

1. Click the Formulas tab.

2. Click the cell you want to trace (this cell must contain a formula) and click the Trace Precedents command.

3. Excel draws tracer arrows to the appropriate cells.

4. Click the Trace Precedents command again to see whether there are any precedents for these calculations.

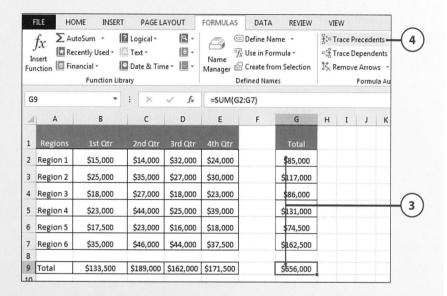

5. If additional precedents are present, Excel draws additional tracer arrows to the appropriate cells.

Removing Formula Auditing Lines References

Click the Remove Arrows command on the Formula tab to remove the arrows.

Checking for Cell References (DEPENDENTS)

When you trace a dependent, you start with a cell referenced in a formula and then trace all cells that reference this cell. This is another way to check whether your formulas are correct. (If the cell is not referenced in a formula, you get an error message saying so.)

1. Click the Formulas tab.

2. Click the cell you want to trace. This cell must not contain a formula.

3. Click the Trace Dependents command until the tracer arrows stop adding on to the appropriate cells.

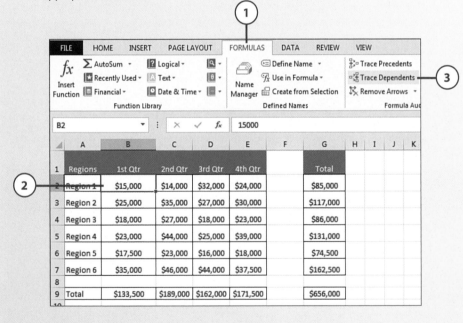

4.   Excel draws tracer arrows to the appropriate cells.

	A	B	C	D	E	F	G	H
1	Regions	1st Qtr	2nd Qtr	3rd Qtr	4th Qtr		Total	
2	Region 1	$15,000	$14,000	$32,000	$24,000		$85,000	
3	Region 2	$25,000	$35,000	$27,000	$30,000		$117,000	
4	Region 3	$18,000	$27,000	$18,000	$23,000		$86,000	
5	Region 4	$23,000	$44,000	$25,000	$39,000		$131,000	
6	Region 5	$17,500	$23,000	$16,000	$18,000		$74,500	
7	Region 6	$35,000	$46,000	$44,000	$37,500		$162,500	
8								4
9	Total	$133,500	$189,000	$162,000	$171,500		$656,000	
10								

5.   Click the Remove Arrows command enough times to remove all the arrows.

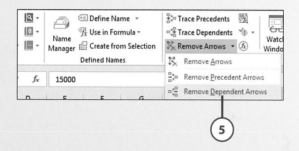

Using Trace Errors

If the cell contains an error message, use the Trace Errors command to have Excel trace possible reasons for the error.

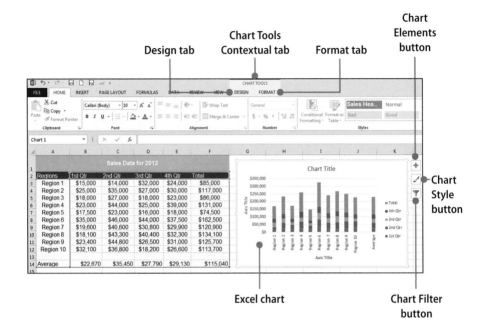

Design tab

Chart Tools Contextual tab

Format tab

Chart Elements button

Chart Style button

Chart Filter button

Excel chart

In this chapter, you discover just how easy it is to create and customize charts in Excel 2013. Topics include the following:

→ Creating a chart
→ Changing the chart type
→ Altering the source data range
→ Altering chart options
→ Formatting the plot and chart areas
→ Formatting the axis scale
→ Altering the original data
→ Adding data to charts
→ Adding a legend

Working with Charts

Charts are graphical representations of data that enable you to visualize and communicate your data in a more meaningful way than with simple numbers in tables. In Excel, you not only have the capability to easily chart your data, but you can also quickly change the appearance of charts with a host of options. For instance, you can change titles, customize the legend, set axis points, add category names, and more.

When working with Excel charts, you see the Chart Tools contextual tab. This tab contains subtabs that expose the various commands you would use to design, layout, and format a chart.

In addition, when you click on a chart, you see several buttons to the right of the chart. These are helper buttons that provide an easy way to customize the various properties of the chart. These include the Chart Elements button, the Chart Style button, and the Chart Filter button.

Creating a Chart

Interpreting numeric data by looking at numbers in a table can be difficult. Using data to create charts can help people visualize the data's significance. For example, you might not have noticed in a spreadsheet that the same month of every year has low sales figures, but it becomes obvious when you make a chart from the data in that spreadsheet. The chart's visual nature also helps others review your data without the need to review every number.

1. Select the cells you want to include in your chart.

2. Click the All Charts dialog launcher at the bottom-right corner of the Charts group on the Ribbon's Insert tab.

3. Select the All Charts tab; then click the Chart Type icon for the chart you want to create.

4. Click the OK button to create your chart.

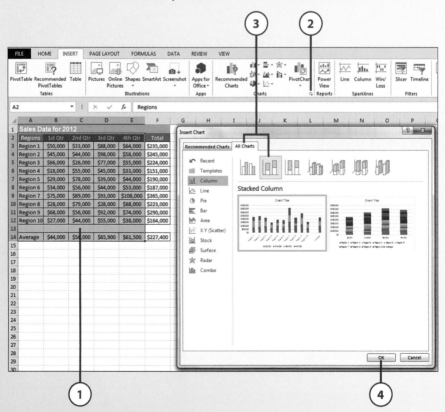

Creating Quick Charts with F11

You can quickly create a chart by selecting your data range and pressing the
F11 key. When you do this, Excel automatically creates a chart and puts it on its
own sheet tab.

5. Click the Quick Layout command to choose a chart layout that includes a chart title.

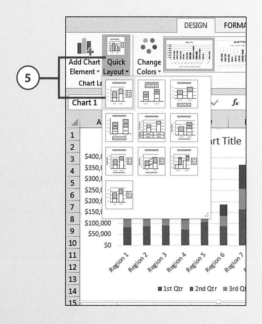

6. Click the Chart Title box, and then type the name for the chart.

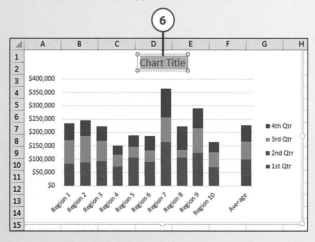

Moving a Chart

Regardless of your selection in step 6, you can always move your chart to another (perhaps new) worksheet. Simply right-click a blank area in the chart and click Move Chart. To place the chart in a new worksheet, click the New Sheet option and type a name for the new sheet. To move it to a different worksheet, click the Object In option button and select the worksheet from the drop-down list. Click OK and Excel moves the chart.

Changing the Chart Type

Charting is one of those skills you learn by doing. At first, you might not even know what type of chart you want to create until you see it. You can always select a different chart type for a chart so that it better represents the data.

1. Click the Change Chart Type command on the Chart Tools Design tab.

2. Select a new chart type and chart subtype in the Change Chart Type dialog box.

3. Click OK.

4. The updated chart type appears in your chart.

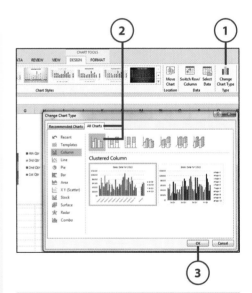

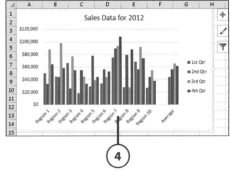

Altering the Source Data Range

Suppose you need to point your chart to a completely different data table. That is to say, the data that will feed your chart will be coming from a different location. In this scenario, you can reconfigure your chart to change its source data location.

1. Click the Select Data command on the Design tab.

2. Click directly in your worksheet and select the new data range. While you're doing this, you see moving dashes around the cells feeding the chart along with the Select Data Source dialog box. After you've selected your new data, press Enter. The Chart Data Range input box in the Select Data Source dialog box automatically updates.

3. Click OK.

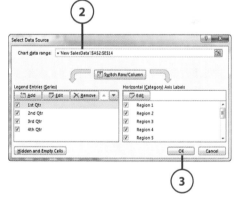

Locating Incorrect Data

If you notice that one of the data points in your chart is way off the scale, this is a good sign that you might have entered data into your worksheet incorrectly. If this is the case, edit the worksheet data and the chart updates automatically. (See the task "Altering the Original Data" later in this chapter for help altering the original data.

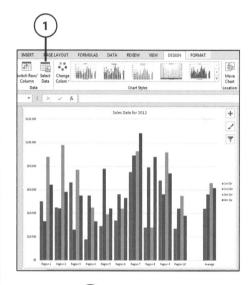

Altering Chart Options

Excel offers you full control over the look and feel of your chart with many customization options. You can add or edit chart titles, alter your axes, add or remove gridlines, move or delete your legend, add or remove data labels, and even show the data table containing your original data. You can manage all this from the helper buttons that activate when you click the chart.

1. Click your chart and choose the Chart Elements button. Then click the arrow next to Chart Title, and choose More Options.

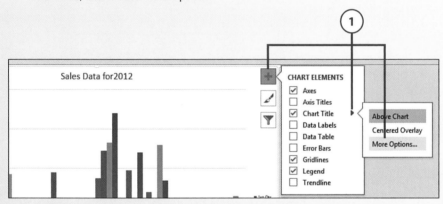

2. Click the arrow next to Fill to expand the Fill section.

3. Add a background color by checking Solid Fill and then choosing a color.

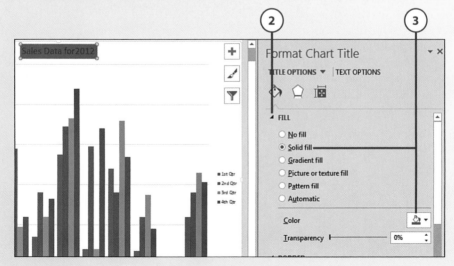

4. Go back to the Chart Elements button, click the arrow next to Axes, and then click More Options.

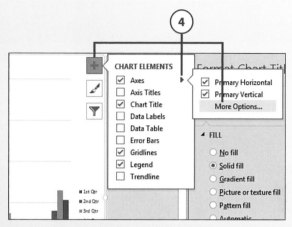

5. Click the Axis Options icon and expand the Numbers section. Customize the number formatting for your Axes here.

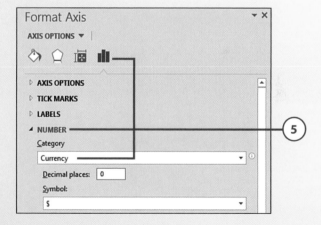

Formatting the Axes Gridlines

To change the pattern and scale of the gridlines, double-click the gridline, and then use the Format Major Gridlines pane to make your selections. Click OK when finished.

6. Go back to the Chart Elements button, and place a check in the Legend property. Click the Legend arrow, and review how altering the placement options affects your chart.

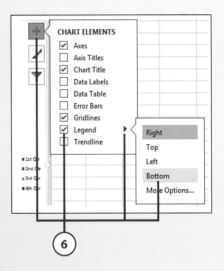

7. Go back to the Chart Elements button, and place a check in the Data Labels property. Click the Data Labels arrow, and review how altering the placement of data labels affects your chart.

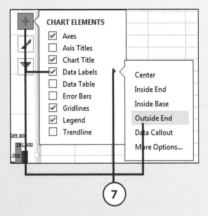

8. Go back to the Chart Elements button, and place a check in the Data Table property. Click the Data Table arrow, and select how you want to show the data table (with or without the legend keys).

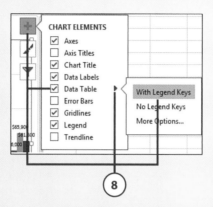

CHART ELEMENTS

- ☑ Axes
- ☐ Axis Titles
- ☑ Chart Title
- ☑ Data Labels
- ☑ Data Table ▶ | With Legend Keys
- ☐ Error Bars   No Legend Keys
- ☑ Gridlines   More Options...
- ☑ Legend
- ☐ Trendline

⑧

9. Review how your chart has changed.

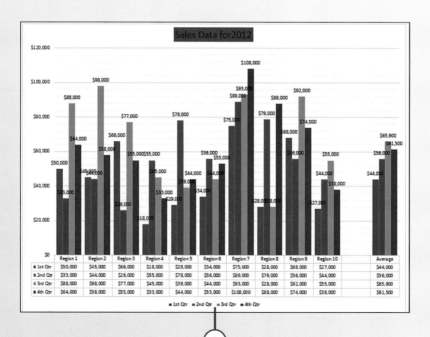

Sales Data for 2012

	Region 1	Region 2	Region 3	Region 4	Region 5	Region 6	Region 7	Region 8	Region 9	Region 10	Average
■ 1st Qtr	$50,000	$45,000	$66,000	$18,000	$29,000	$34,000	$75,000	$28,000	$68,000	$27,000	$44,000
■ 2nd Qtr	$33,000	$44,000	$26,000	$55,000	$78,000	$56,000	$89,000	$79,000	$56,000	$44,000	$56,000
■ 3rd Qtr	$88,000	$98,000	$77,000	$45,000	$39,000	$44,000	$93,000	$28,000	$92,000	$55,000	$65,900
■ 4th Qtr	$64,000	$58,000	$55,000	$33,000	$44,000	$53,000	$108,000	$88,000	$74,000	$38,000	$61,500

■ 1st Qtr ■ 2nd Qtr ■ 3rd Qtr ■ 4th Qtr

⑨

>>>Go Further

CUSTOMIZE YOUR CHARTS APPROPRIATELY

There are literally hundreds of different customization options; too many to include in this book. In reality, you wouldn't use more than a handful on any given chart. Why?

The final chart shown for the "Altering Chart Options" task looks busy—even ugly. Of course, the example chart given here was designed to show you the mechanics of adding several customizations to your chart. But as you can see in the final result, overzealous use of chart customizations can lead to ineffective charts.

Your goal when creating a chart is not to jam in as many bells and whistles as possible. The goal of your chart is to make use of these customizations in such a way as to best relay your message.

Printing Charts

You can print a chart just like you print anything else in Excel. If you want to print just your chart (as opposed to the entire worksheet) select the chart, click the File tab on the Ribbon, and select the Print option.

Formatting the Plot Area

The *plot area* consists of a border and the location of the data points in your chart. You can alter the style, color, and weight of the border. You can also alter the color of the plot area.

1. Click the Chart Elements drop-down on the Format tab; then choose Plot Area from the drop-down.

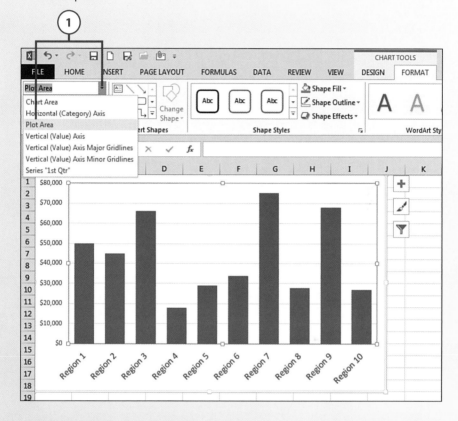

2. Click the Shape Fill button, and then choose a color to change the background color of the plot area.

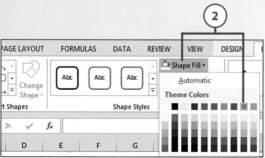

3. Observe how your chart has changed.

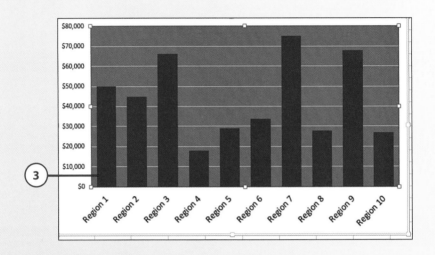

Determining Which Area You're In

If you are unsure whether you are in the chart area or the plot area, click directly on the chart. Look at the Chart Elements drop-down in the upper-left corner of the Format tab. This drop-down shows the name of the chart element that is currently active. You can also use this nifty drop-down to quickly switch from one element to another.

Formatting the Chart Area

The *chart area* consists of a border, the background, and all the chart fonts. You can alter the style, color, and weight of the border. You can also alter the color of the background. You can also change all the fonts and font styles in the chart.

1. Click the Chart Elements drop-down on the Format tab; then choose Chart Area from the drop-down.

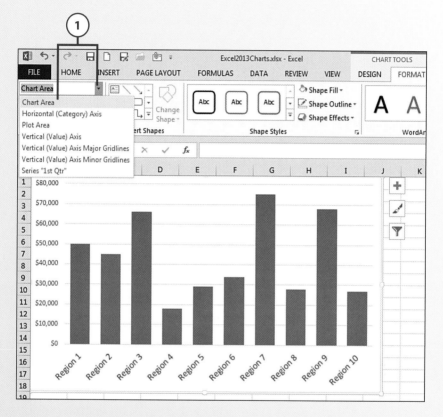

2. Click the Shape Fill button, and then choose a color to change the background color of the plot area.

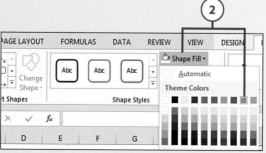

3. Observe how your chart has changed.

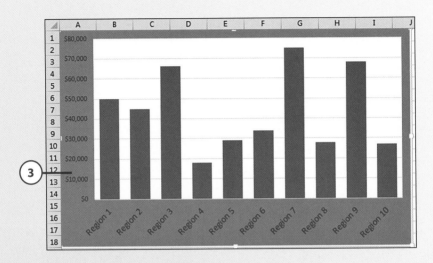

Formatting from the Home Tab

You can change the font and color of most chart elements by using the formatting commands on the Home tab. You can simply select the chart element and then go to the Home tab to easily change the font, alignment, color, and other format properties. This makes quick work of any formatting tasks you need to do on your charts.

Formatting the Axis Scale

Excel automatically establishes the axis increments according to the maximum amount on the chart. Usually, this will suffice, but if you want to show more detail about actual numbers, it can be convenient to alter your value axis.

1. Click the Chart Elements drop-down on the Format tab; then choose Vertical (Value) Axis from the drop-down. Click the Format Selection command.

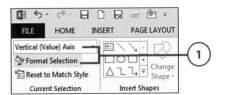

2. Click the Axis Options icon, and type the changes to the axis scale increments—for example, decrease the value in the Major unit field.

3. Review how your chart has changed.

Number Formatting and Alignment

To change the number format, expand the Number section on the Axis Options pane, and select the numeric format you want to use. To change the alignment of the axis so that they are vertical, click Text Options in the dialog box shown in step 2, and select a rotation for the axes under the Textbox section.

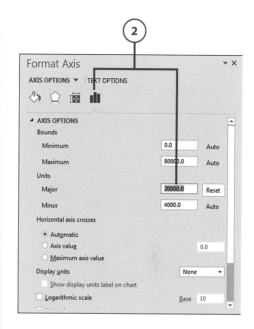

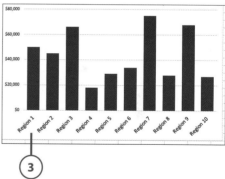

Altering the Original Data

A chart is linked to the worksheet data, so when you make a change in the worksheet, the chart is updated. If you want to change a value in the worksheet, edit it as you do normally. The chart is instantly updated to reflect the change. If you delete data in the worksheet, the matching data series is deleted in the chart.

1. Select the worksheet tab or range that contains the charted data.

2. Click a cell that you want to alter or need to update.

3. Type the new data and press the Enter key.

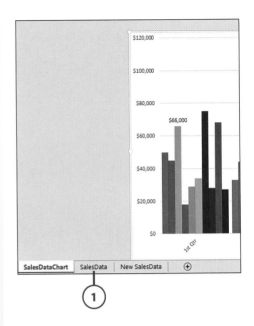

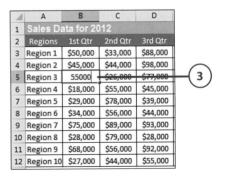

4. Go back to the chart and see how the edited data point has changed your chart.

Saving Changes

When working with charts, you want to make sure you save your changes often. You wouldn't want to lose any changes you made in case your network goes down or your computer freezes.

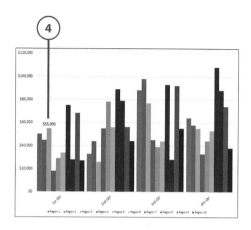

Adding Data to Charts

Suppose you want to expand your chart to include additional data. If so, you need to place the data on your original worksheet and indicate to Excel that you want it included in your chart.

1. After adding any new data you want to include in your chart to the original data range, click directly on your chart to see what data is currently referenced in the chart.

2. Click and drag the blue chart data line to include the newly added data.

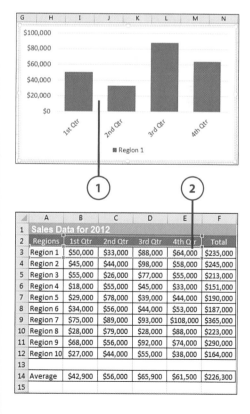

	A	B	C	D	E	F
1	Sales Data for 2012					
2	Regions	1st Qtr	2nd Qtr	3rd Qtr	4th Qtr	Total
3	Region 1	$50,000	$33,000	$88,000	$64,000	$235,000
4	Region 2	$45,000	$44,000	$98,000	$58,000	$245,000
5	Region 3	$55,000	$26,000	$77,000	$55,000	$213,000
6	Region 4	$18,000	$55,000	$45,000	$33,000	$151,000
7	Region 5	$29,000	$78,000	$39,000	$44,000	$190,000
8	Region 6	$34,000	$56,000	$44,000	$53,000	$187,000
9	Region 7	$75,000	$89,000	$93,000	$108,000	$365,000
10	Region 8	$28,000	$79,000	$28,000	$88,000	$223,000
11	Region 9	$68,000	$56,000	$92,000	$74,000	$290,000
12	Region 10	$27,000	$44,000	$55,000	$38,000	$164,000
13						
14	Average	$42,900	$56,000	$65,900	$61,500	$226,300
15						

3. Use the blue handle to drag the chart data line in the new location.

4. The chart automatically updates to include the new data.

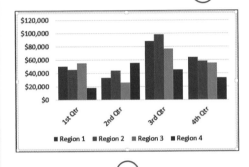

⬚	A	B	C	D	E	F
1	Sales Data for 2012					
2	Regions	1st Qtr	2nd Qtr	3rd Qtr	4th Qtr	Total
3	Region 1	$50,000	$33,000	$88,000	$64,000	$235,000
4	Region 2	$45,000	$44,000	$98,000	$58,000	$245,000
5	Region 3	$55,000	$26,000	$77,000	$55,000	$213,000
6	Region 4	$18,000	$55,000	$45,000	$33,000	$151,000
7	Region 5	$29,000	$78,000	$39,000	$44,000	$190,000
8	Region 6	$34,000	$56,000	$44,000	$53,000	$187,000

Excluding Chart Data

You can also click and drag the blue chart data line to exclude data in your chart. Simply drag the blue line so that the data you want to exclude is no longer contained within the chart.

Adding a Legend

A *legend* helps a reader make sense of all the data points and colors shown in a chart. You typically don't need a legend if you're only plotting one data series. However, if you are plotting two or more data series in one chart, it's definitely a best practice to have a legend. Considering that you will probably add data to your chart, going from one data series to many, it's helpful to know how to add a legend after your chart has been created.

1. Click anywhere on your chart.

2. Click the Chart Elements Button.

3. Click the checkbox next to the Legend property.

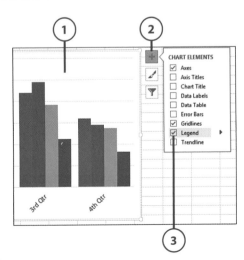

4. Note that your chart now has a Legend.

Quickly Formatting Legends

Right-click the legend and choose Format Legend from the shortcut menu. From the dialog box that appears, you can alter the patterns, fonts, and even the placement of the legend.

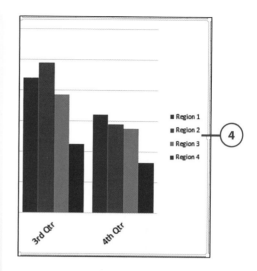

An example
of WordArt

An example of
a picture file

An example
of ClipArt

An example of
an object (Word
document)

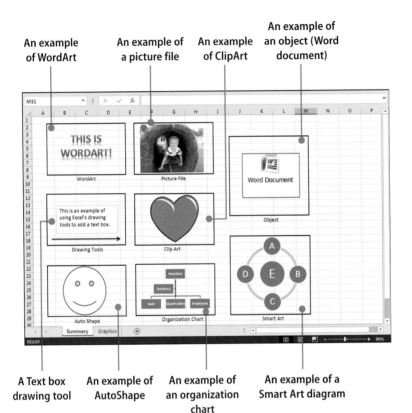

A Text box
drawing tool

An example of
AutoShape

An example of
an organization
chart

An example of a
Smart Art diagram

In this chapter, you discover the ins and outs of creating and customizing your own graphics in Excel. Topics include the following:

→ Using drawing tools
→ Inserting clip art
→ Inserting a picture from a file
→ Using AutoShapes
→ Inserting WordArt
→ Inserting objects
→ Working with inserted objects

7

Working with Graphics

There might be instances when you're asked to add graphics to your Excel worksheets. For example, you might need to insert your company's logo on each worksheet you create. Well, the good news is that Excel has a whole host of tools that enable you to create and customize your own graphics and visualizations. With these tools, you can add a picture from another file, draw pictures, insert shapes, use ClipArt, and create your own WordArt.

Using Drawing Tools

Excel has drawing tools that you can use to draw on a worksheet or chart. In this task, you discover the advantages of using Excel drawing tools to point out information on a worksheet.

1. Click the Shapes drop-down on the Insert tab.

2. Click any of the drawing tool buttons—for example, the Arrow. The mouse pointer turns into a plus sign.

3. Click and drag in the worksheet to draw an arrow; release the mouse button when the arrow is the length you want it to be. (The pointer end is at the point of release.)

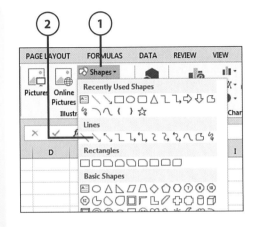

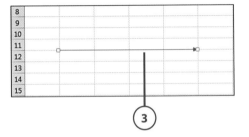

Quick Color and Style

If you click on any shape, you see a new Drawing Tools Format tab. There, you can apply some predefined styles for your shapes by choosing a style from the Shape Styles gallery.

Using AutoShapes

The Shapes Command (on the Insert tab) includes tools for drawing common shapes, such as lines, circles, squares, and so on. If you aren't much of an artist or if you want to try some prefab symbols, insert an AutoShape. You can select from several lines, connectors, basic shapes, arrows, flowchart symbols, stars, callouts, banners, and more.

4. Click the Text Box command on the Insert tab. The mouse pointer turns into an insertion pointer.

5. Click and drag in the worksheet to draw a text box; release the mouse button when the box is the size you want it to be.

6. Type the text you want to enter in the text box.

7. Click anywhere outside the text box to see how it looks.

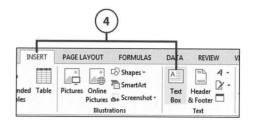

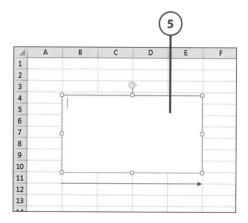

Text Boxes

The benefit of using text boxes is that you can move, resize, and format them to suit your needs. This is an excellent alternative to formatting a cell in a worksheet where real estate can be limited.

Modifying Drawing Objects

A drawn object is just like a picture—you can edit it as needed. To resize a drawn object, click the object and then drag the sizing handles to the size you want and release the mouse button. To move the object, click the object and drag it to the wanted location in the worksheet. To delete an object, click the object and press the Delete key on the keyboard.

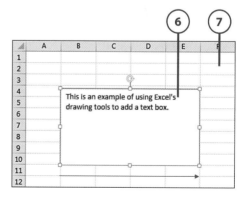

Inserting Clip Art

Clip art adds visual interest to your Excel worksheets. With Microsoft clip art, you can choose from numerous professionally prepared images, sounds, and movie clips. After you add graphics, you can move them around in the worksheet and even assign text wrapping.

1. Click the Online Pictures button on the Insert tab to open the Insert Pictures task pane.

2. Type a description for the clip art you are looking for in the Search for text box and press Enter. (Or click the Go button, which is not shown in the figure.)

3. If Microsoft has clip art that matches the description you type, it displays in the Insert Pictures task pane. Click an image in the results list, and then click Insert to add it to your worksheet.

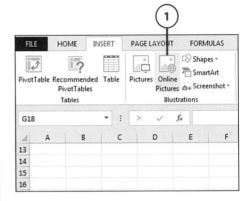

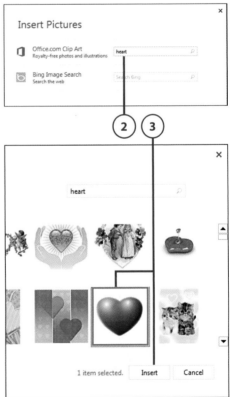

4. The clip art is inserted into your worksheet. (You might need to move or resize the image; see the tasks "Move an Object" and "Resize an Object.")

The Picture Tools Format Tab

If you click on any picture or clip art, you see a new Picture Tools Format tab. There, you find tools to crop, format, adjust contrast, apply effects, and most anything else you would typically do to a picture.

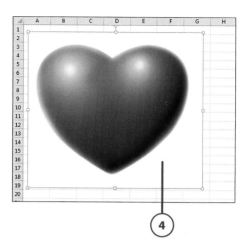

Inserting a Picture from File

Often, you want to embed your own company approved pictures into your worksheet. A good example of this is a company logo. Excel is quite flexible and enables you to insert varying types of picture files: bitmap files, JPEG files, PNG files, TIF files, PCX files, and many more.

1. Click the Pictures button on the Insert tab to open the Insert Picture dialog box.

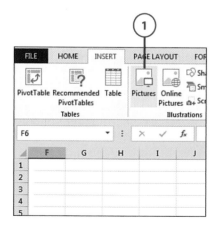

2. Locate the file you want to use and click it to see a preview. (You might need to select Preview from the dialog box Views button).

3. Click the Insert button.

4. The image is inserted into your worksheet.

Manage Overlapping Picture Objects

If you have multiple pictures on your worksheet, you can manage how the pictures overlap each other. Simply right-click each picture, and select either Send to Back or Bring to Front. This way, you can better control the layout of your pictures—and even layer your pictures to create robust visualizations.

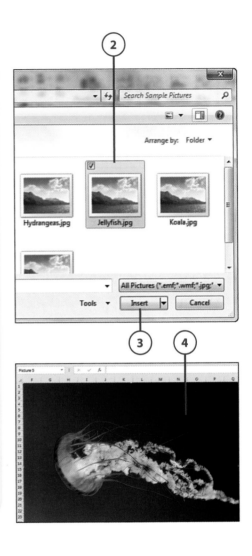

Using AutoShapes

Excel enables you to add numerous predesigned shapes, called AutoShapes, to your worksheets. For example, you can insert any one of the following AutoShapes into your worksheet: Lines, Connectors, Basic Shapes, Block Arrows, Flowchart, Stars and Banners, Callouts, and more. AutoShapes are ideal when you don't want to spend the time to draw your own fancy symbols.

1. Click the Shapes drop-down on the Insert tab, and select from the different shape options (here, Smiley Face).

2. The mouse pointer changes to a plus sign. Click and drag the pointer to draw the object at the wanted size; then release the mouse button.

3. The new shape is added, complete with sizing handles.

Resizing and Moving Objects

Move the mouse over an object border; the pointer becomes a four-headed arrow, and you can move it (see the "Move an Object" task); a two-headed arrow enables you to resize it (see the "Resize an Object" task).

Formatting AutoShapes

To format your AutoShape, right-click the object and select Format Shape from the shortcut menu. Click the Fill & Line tab; then choose from the various fills, line types, and arrows. You can also use the Format tab that appears on the ribbon after you select an AutoShape.

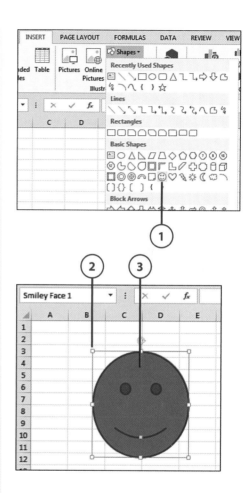

Inserting WordArt

WordArt is a text-based object that Microsoft provides to apply special effects to text. You don't have to add these text effects manually; the different styles of WordArt are indeed the text effects themselves.

1. Click the Text button on the Insert tab; then click the WordArt button to open the WordArt Gallery.

2. Click the WordArt style you want to use to insert it onto the worksheet.

3. Type your text into the Text box placed on the worksheet and press Enter.

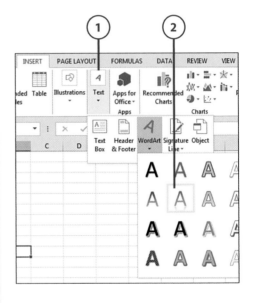

Formatting WordArt

After your WordArt is inserted into your worksheet, the Drawing Tools Format tab appears on the Ribbon (while the WordArt object is selected). You can use the Drawing Tools Format tab to edit the text, alter the style, format the text, and add more WordArt.

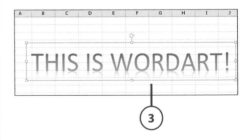

Using Smart Art in Excel

Smart Art is often described as representation of information and ideas. You can think of Smart Art as a way to visually communicate concepts that are difficult to communicate with data alone. For example, it would be difficult to build a data table that effectively communicates an organization's hierarchy. This is where Smart Art comes in.

1. Click SmartArt on the Insert tab.

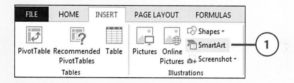

2. Click Organization Chart under the Hierarchy category.

3. Click OK to insert the new SmartArt into your worksheet.

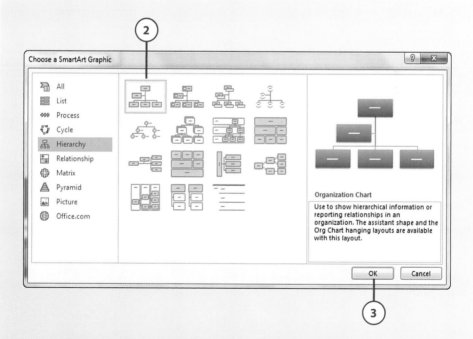

4. An organization chart containing dummy text is inserted into your worksheet. To fill the chart in yourself, click a text box and type over the dummy text with your own text.

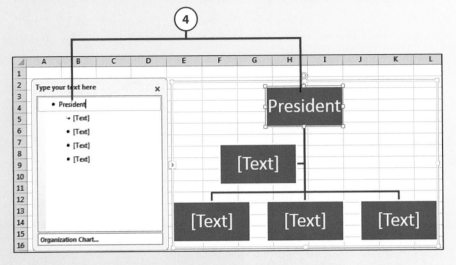

5. The SmartArt Tools tabs offer options, such as adding a subordinate, co-worker, or assistant, to the selected text box. For example, you can click the drop-down next to the Add Shape button and click Add Assistant.

The SmartArt Tools Format Tab

After you add a SmartArt graphic you see a SmartArt Tools Format tab. There, you can find tools to alter the SmartArt, add effects, change color, and many other customizations.

Inserting a Diagram

Diagrams are ideal when you need to illustrate and communicate a workflow, process, or other conceptual paradigms with your spreadsheet data. You can insert the diagram and then add the appropriate information.

1. On the Insert tab, click the SmartArt button to display the Choose a SmartArt Graphic dialog box.

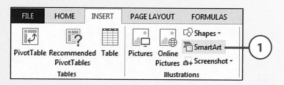

2. Click the wanted diagram type; a diagram of that type containing dummy text is inserted into your worksheet.

3. Click OK.

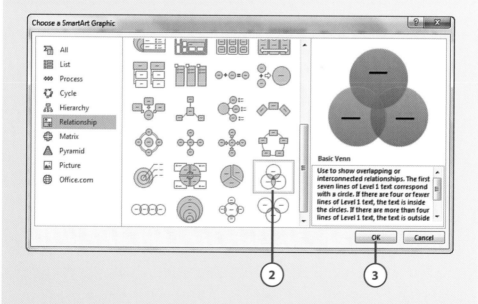

4. Click each instance of dummy text and replace it with text of your own.

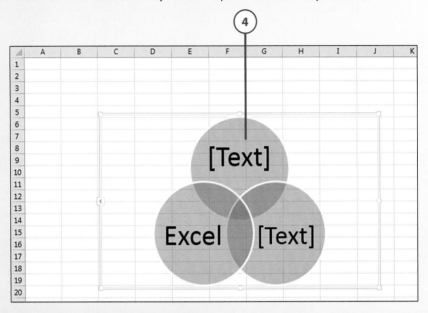

Using the Layouts Gallery

After your diagram is in place, use the Layouts gallery under the Design tab to try out different layouts. Excel keeps all your text and settings but shows your diagram in a different layout. Often, you'll find one that better illustrates your message than the one you originally selected.

Inserting Objects

In addition to inserting all the different types of graphic objects covered in this chapter, you can also insert objects that aren't as commonly added to Excel worksheets. For example, you can insert a media clip, PowerPoint slide, Microsoft Works chart, video clip, and much more.

1. Click the Object button on the Insert tab to open the Object dialog box.

2. Scroll through the Object type list; double-click the object you want to insert—for example, Microsoft Word Document.

3. Edit the object according to the individual object properties as you would when creating a Word document.

Getting to the Object Properties

After your object is on your spreadsheet, you can edit the object by right-clicking it and selecting Document Object. This displays a submenu: Edit, Open, Convert. Using these menu options, you can edit the object source, open the object itself, or convert the object so that it displays as an icon.

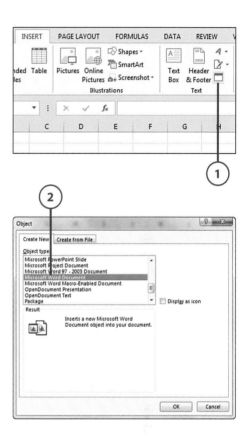

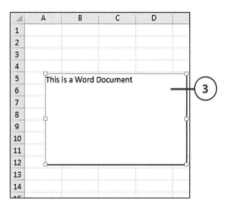

Working with Inserted Objects

As you have seen, you can add charts to a worksheet, draw objects, insert pictures, and more. Each of these items exists on a separate layer on top of the worksheet and is generically called an object. As you discover in the next several tasks, you can format, move, resize, and delete objects. First, however, you must select the object you want to modify.

1. Click the object you want to select; selection handles appear around the edges of the object.

2. Move the mouse over the object border; the pointer becomes a four-headed arrow that you can use to move; a two-headed arrow enables you to resize it.

Selecting Multiple Objects

To select multiple objects, click the first object, press and hold down the Ctrl key, and click the second object. Continue until you select all the objects you want.

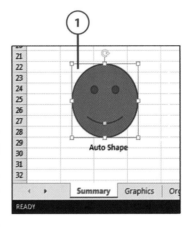

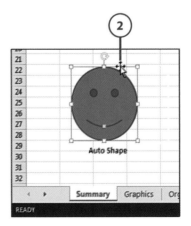

Format an Object

You can format objecsts just as easily as you format text, data, and worksheets. Depending on the object, the standard formatting options you can change are as follows: font (text changes in the object), alignment (where text aligns in the object), colors and lines (whether lines are filled, colored, or have arrows), size (the height, width, and scale of the object), protection (whether others can alter your object), properties (how you position the object and whether you can print it), and Web (text to display while the object loads online).

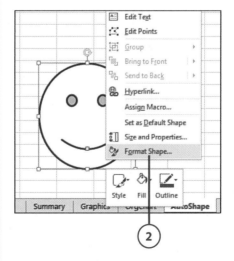

1. Right-click the object you want to format; selection handles appear around the edges of the object.

2. Select Format *object name* from the shortcut menu (where *object name* is the type of object you have selected). The Format *object name* dialog box opens.

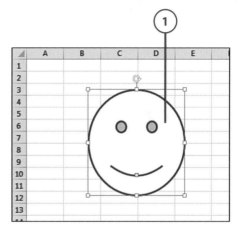

3. Alter the formatting options as needed and click Close.

4. The formatting changes are applied to the object.

Double-Click to the Format Dialog Box

You can also double-click the object to automatically open the Format dialog box associated with it.

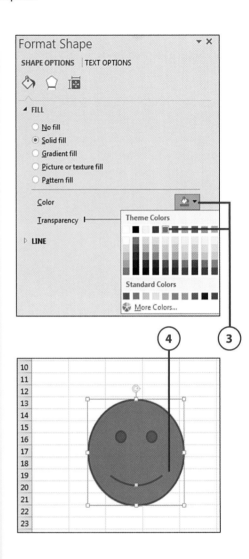

Move an Object

When you draw an object on or add an object to a worksheet, you might not like its placement. Perhaps the object obscures the worksheet data, or maybe it needs to be moved a little closer to (or farther away from) the data. Fortunately, you can easily move an object.

1. Select the object you want to move; selection handles appear around the edges of the object.

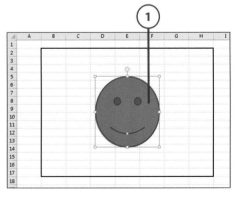

2. Click directly on the object or its border (not the selection handles) and hold the left mouse button while dragging the object to the new location.

3. Release the mouse button to drop the object in the new location. The object is moved.

Copying Objects

To copy an object, press and hold down the Ctrl key on your keyboard as you drag; a copy of the original object is moved to the new location, and the original remains intact where it is.

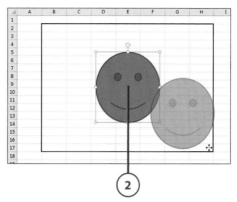

2

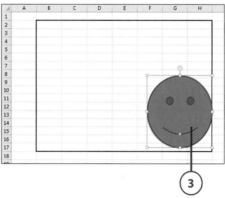

3

Moving an Object to Another Worksheet

You can move your target object to a separate worksheet by following these simple steps. First, right-click the target object and select Cut. Move to the new sheet, right-click the spot where you want the object to appear, and then select Paste. You can also use these steps to move your object to a different workbook.

Remember to use the Ctrl+X (Cut) and Ctrl+V (Paste) shortcut keys to save time.

Resize an Object

If an object is too big (or too small), change the size. You can resize any type of object, including a picture, chart, or drawn object you added. In addition, you can continue to resize the object over and over until it is the size you want.

1. Select the object you want to resize; selection handles appear around the edges of the object.

2. Move the pointer over one of the selection handles (here, a corner handle). When the pointer is in the right spot, it changes to a two-headed arrow.

3. Click the handle, drag it, and release the mouse button when the object is the wanted size.

4. The object is resized.

Corners Versus Sides

Dragging the sides increases or decreases the height or width of an object, whereas dragging the corners increases or decreases the height and width of an object at the same time.

Resizing Proportionally

If you hold the Shift key down while dragging a corner, the image enlarges or decreases in proportion.

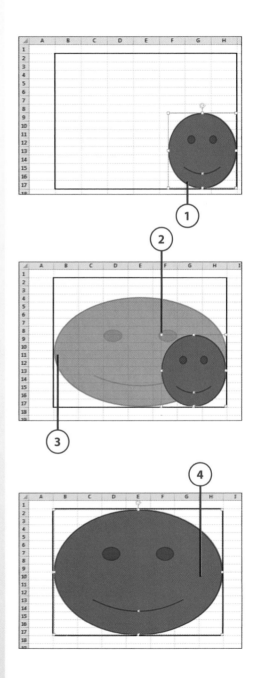

Delete an Object

As you experiment with charts, drawings, and pictures, you might go overboard, or you might make a mistake and want to start over. In any case, if you add an object and no longer want to include it, you can delete it, as described here.

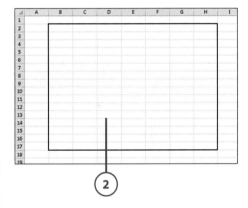

1. Select the object you want to delete; selection handles appear around the edges of the object.

2. Press the Delete key on your keyboard. Excel deletes the object.

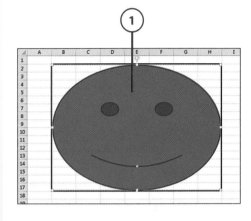

Undoing a Deletion

If you accidentally delete an object, click the Undo button on the Quick Access Toolbar to undo the deletion. Alternatively, you can use the Ctrl+Z shortcut on your keyboard.

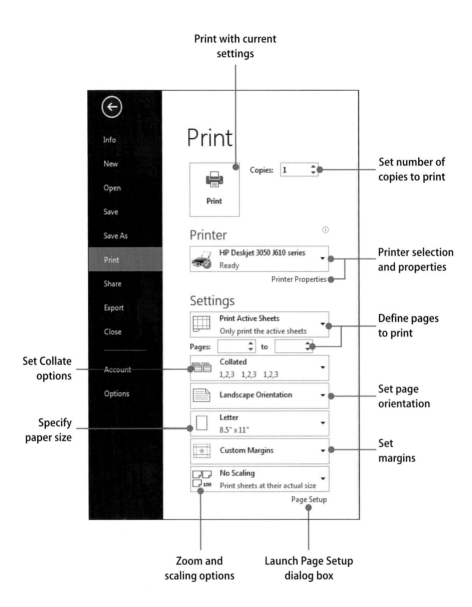

Print with current settings

Set number of copies to print

Printer selection and properties

Define pages to print

Set page orientation

Set margins

Set Collate options

Specify paper size

Zoom and scaling options

Launch Page Setup dialog box

In this chapter, you get a tour of the printing options available to you in Excel 2013. Topics in this chapter include the following:

→ Using Print Preview
→ Setting the print area and margins
→ Using page breaks
→ Centering and printing a worksheet on one page
→ Printing in portrait or landscape orientation
→ Printing gridlines, cell comments, and error indicators
→ Printing repeating row labels and column headers
→ Adding headers and footers

Printing in Excel

Printing options in Excel haven't changed much since Excel 2003. However, Excel 2013 does consolidate most printing options into the Backstage view. At this point in the book, you should know that you can get to the Backstage view by clicking the File tab on the Ribbon. Although there are several methods to get to the print options, Excel 2013's Backstage view provides an easy way to quickly configure them.

Excel enables you to print your worksheets by using basic print settings if that's all you need. But Excel also offers a bunch of settings that enable you to enhance your printouts. Some of these options include orientation adjustments, scaling, paper size options, page numbering, adding headers, adding footers, and much more.

Using Print Preview

Worksheets with lots of data can generate large print jobs, possibly containing hundreds of pages. Waiting until all pages are printed to verify that the information is printed correctly can cost a lot in both time and printing supplies. To help prevent printing mistakes, use Print Preview to ensure that all the necessary elements appear on the pages before printing.

1. With the worksheet you want to print open, click the File tab on the Ribbon.

2. Click Print to display the worksheet's Print Preview.

Paging Through the Print Preview
The navigation spinner is in the lower-left corner of the Print Preview. In this case, the navigation spinner reads 1 of 2. You not only can use this to determine how many pages will be printed, but you can also cycle through the pages by clicking the left and right arrows.

Page Break Preview Button
Click Page Break Preview on the View Tab to see and modify exactly what is selected to print (in the print area). If you haven't set the print area, see "Setting the Print Area."

3. Click the Zoom button to increase the viewable size of the worksheet in Print Preview mode. (Click Zoom again to return to the original page size.)

4. Click Margins to toggle between displaying the margin indicators, which you can drag to set more or less of your worksheet to print.

5. Click the Back button to return to the worksheet's Normal view.

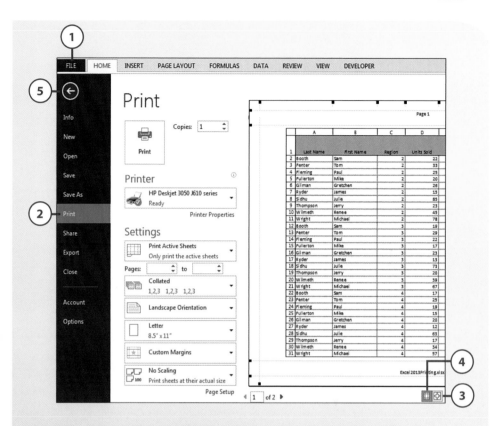

Zoom with Your Mouse Wheel

If you have a mouse wheel (a wheel in the center of your mouse between the left and right clicks) you have another quick way to zoom. Hold down the Ctrl key on your keyboard while you spin your mouse wheel. The direction you spin (up or down) increases or reduces magnification in Print Preview.

Setting the Print Area

Worksheets can include several rows and columns; setting the print area enables you to specify which rows and columns to print. If you don't set a print area, all cells that contain data will print. You can limit your print job to a certain range of cells.

1. Select the exact cells you want to print.

2. Click the Page Layout tab.

3. Click the Print Area command on the Ribbon and select Set Print Area. This stores the print area as part of the worksheet. Now, only the cells in the print area print.

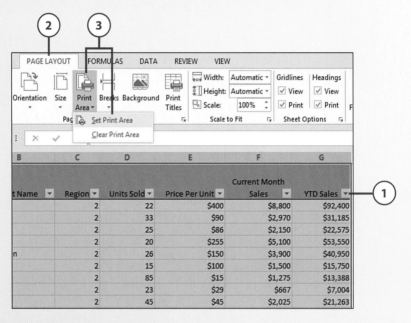

Long and Short Dashes

The long dashed lines in your worksheet indicate the print area, and the smaller dashed lines indicate the current page margins. If your print area data falls outside the current page margins, you need to alter the page margins.

Clearing the Print Area

You might find that you need to set the print area to print specific cells, but only as a one-time task. In these scenarios, you want to clear the print area after you print. Go to the Page Layout tab, click the Print Area command, and select Clear Print Area.

Adjusting Page Margins

Margins affect where data is printed on a page. They also determine where headers and footers are printed. Occasionally, you might need to change margins to make room for a letterhead or logo on preprinted stationery. When in Print Preview mode, Excel enables you to simultaneously alter your margins.

1. With the worksheet you want to print open, click the File tab on the Ribbon.

2. Click Print to display the worksheet's Print Preview.

3. Click the Margins button.

4. Drag the Margin lines to the position you need them.

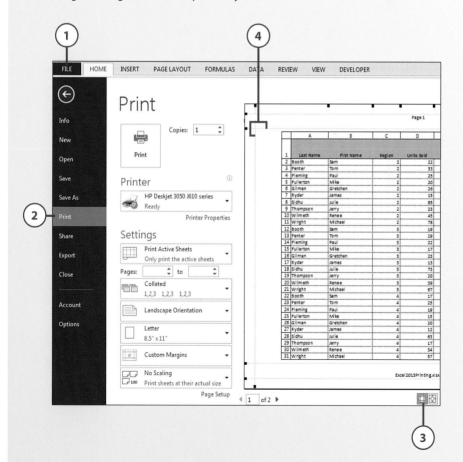

Entering Specific Margins

The steps in this task are ideal if you want to merely adjust or tweak your margins. If, however, you need to enter specific margin measurements, the Page Setup dialog box is a better option. Go to the Page Layout tab and click the Page Setup dialog launcher. In the Page Setup dialog box, you can click the Margins tab and alter the margins (Left, Right, Top, Bottom, Header, and Footer) as necessary. Click OK to return to your worksheet or Print to print immediately.

Inserting Page Breaks

When a worksheet page is filled to the margins with data, Excel automatically inserts a page break for you. There might be times, however, when you want to manually insert a page break. For example, if you create a report with multiple topic sections, you might want each topic to begin on a new page. Inserting a page break enables you to print each page separately. The best way to insert page breaks is using Page Break Preview view (instead of Normal view).

1. Open the View tab and choose Page Break Preview to change to Page Break Preview mode.

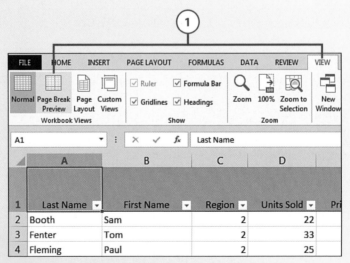

2. Click the cell below and click in the leftmost column in which you want to insert a page break.

3. On the Page Layout tab, choose Breaks and then Insert Page Break to insert the page break.

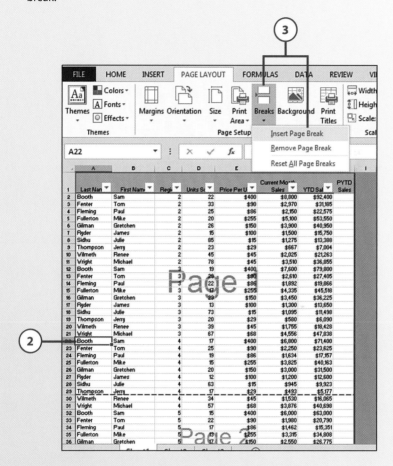

4. The page break is inserted.

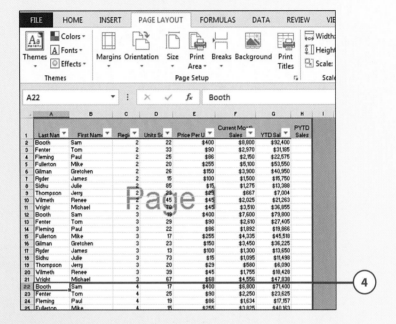

Removing Page Breaks

To remove a page break, place the active cell so that one of the cell borders is touching the page break line. On the Page Layout tab, click Breaks and then Remove Page Break. (You can also do this in Normal view.)

Page Break Intersection

A page break is always inserted as an intersection between rows and columns. If the active cell isn't in the first column, the page break is inserted as four quadrants.

Why Not Simply Add More Rows?

Suppose you want each of two tables that fit on one page to print on separate pages. Instead of inserting a page break, you could add several blank rows to the end of the first table, which automatically kicks the second one onto a second page. If, however, you later add any rows to the first table and forget to delete the same number of blank rows before the second one, the tables might not print correctly.

Working in Page Break Preview Mode

Page Break Preview mode displays the area you have selected for your set print area. It also enables you to click and drag where your page breaks are instead of using the Insert, Page Break command. You can also edit the text and data just as you can in Normal view.

1. Click Page Break Preview from the View tab on the Ribbon. If a print area has been set, it displays; if not, the entire worksheet displays.

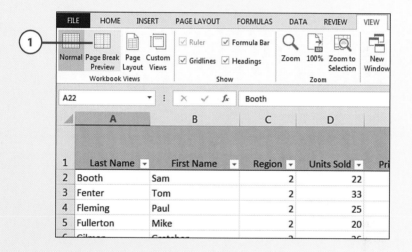

2. To move a page break that is poorly placed, click and drag it to a better location.

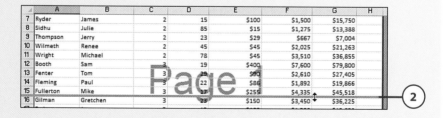

3. To exclude a column or data to the right of your set print area, click and drag the vertical page break.

	A	B	C	D	E	F	G	H
7	Ryder	James	2	15	$100	$1,500	$15,750	
8	Sidhu	Julie	2	85	$15	$1,275	$13,388	
9	Thompson	Jerry	2	23	$29	$667	$7,004	
10	Wilmeth	Renee	2	45	$45	$2,025	$21,263	
11	Wright	Michael	2	78	$45	$3,510	$36,855	
12	Booth	Sam	3	19	$400	$7,600	$79,800	
13	Fenter	Tom	3	29	$90	$2,610	$27,405	
14	Fleming	Paul	3	22	$86	$1,892	$19,866	
15	Fullerton	Mike	3	17	$255	$4,335	$45,518	
16	Gilman	Gretchen	3	23	$150	$3,450	$36,225	
17	Ryder	James	3	13	$100	$1,300	$13,650	
18	Sidhu	Julie	3	73	$15	$1,095	$11,498	
19	Thompson	Jerry	3	20	$29	$580	$6,090	
20	Wilmeth	Renee	3	39	$45	$1,755	$18,428	
21	Wright	Michael	3	67	$68	$4,556	$47,838	
22	Booth	Sam	4	17	$400	$6,800	$71,400	
23	Fenter	Tom	4	25	$90	$2,250	$23,625	
24	Fleming	Paul	4	19	$86	$1,634	$17,157	

③

Natural Versus Inserted Page Breaks

Naturally occurring page breaks appear as blue dashed lines, whereas page breaks that you insert appear as solid blue lines. Moving a natural page break automatically changes it to a solid blue line.

Removing a Page Break

To remove a page break in Page Break Preview mode, click and drag the page break line off to the right/left/top/bottom of the worksheet.

Printing a Worksheet on One Page

By default, Excel prints your worksheet at a scale of 100 percent. You can decrease this percentage if you want to fit more data on a page or increase it to fit less data on a page. In addition, you can have Excel fit your entire worksheet on one page. (If your worksheet is large, the data might become too tiny to read when scaled down.)

1. With the worksheet you want to print open, click the File tab on the Ribbon.

2. Click Print to display the worksheet's Print Preview.

3. Click the Zoom and Scaling drop-down (the button that reads No Scaling).

4. Select the Fit Sheet on One Page option.

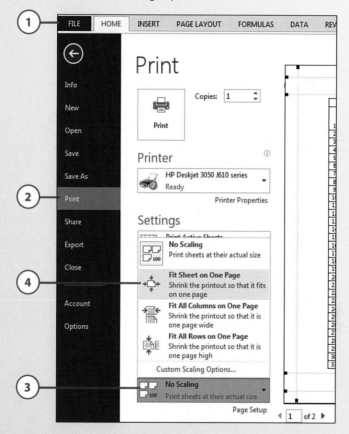

Changing from Letter to Legal

To choose a different paper size for your printout, click the Paper Size drop-down (the button that reads Letter) on the Print pane of the Backstage View. There, you can select Legal. The scaling setting automatically adjusts to the selected paper size.

Returning to the Default Scale

When you want to return the preview of your worksheet to the default scale, return the Zoom and Scaling drop-down and set it back to the No Scaling option.

Printing in Portrait or Landscape Orientation

Not all Excel reports are the same. Some reports have just a few columns, whereas others are wide with many columns. Depending on your report, you either print in Portrait or Landscape orientation. The default orientation in Excel is Portrait— meaning the report can fit vertically on one page without the sides being cut off. Landscape orientation means that your page is printed horizontally (on its side) so that you get that extra room on the sides so that all your columns fit.

1. With the worksheet you want to print open, click the File tab on the Ribbon.

2. Click Print to display the worksheet's Print Preview.

3. Click the Portrait Orientation drop-down.

4. Select the Landscape Orientation option.

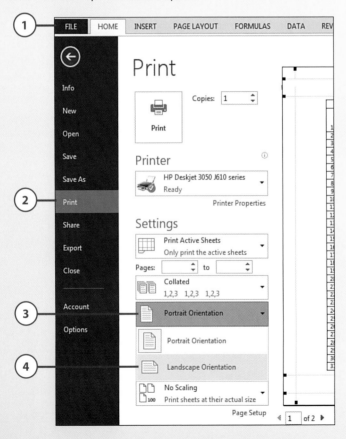

Using the Orientation Ribbon Command

Alternatively, you can switch between landscape and portrait by using the Orientation drop-down button on the Page Layout tab.

Centering a Worksheet on a Page

If you want a cleaner, more professional-looking printout for a presentation, you might want to center your worksheet data on the page before you print it. This is a particularly good idea if you plan to print your worksheet on one page.

1. Click the Page Layout tab.

2. Click the Page Setup dialog launcher.

3. On the Margins tab, click the Horizontally and/or Vertically check boxes in the Center on Page area.

4. Click OK.

Centering Vertically or Horizontally

You don't need to center your data both vertically and horizontally. You can choose one or the other, depending on how you want your printed worksheet to look.

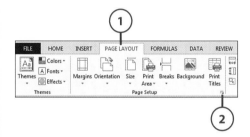

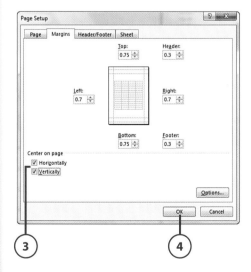

Printing Gridlines and Row/Column Headers

By default, Excel doesn't print worksheet gridlines or row/column headers. You can, however, instruct Excel to print them. Gridlines help you read information in a printed worksheet, keeping rows and columns of data visually organized. Row and column headers can help you quickly find data in your worksheet.

1. Click the Page Layout tab.

2. Click the Page Setup dialog launcher.

3. On the Sheet tab, click the Gridlines and Row and Column Headings check boxes in the Print area to select them.

4. Click OK.

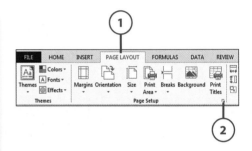

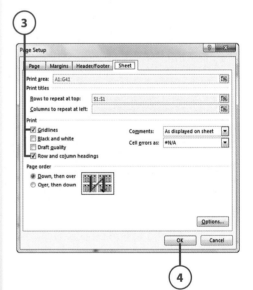

Repeating Titles

Displaying row and column headers is not the same as printing repeating titles. Repeating titles are column headers and row headers that you have assigned in your worksheet. For more information, see the task "Printing Repeating Row and Column Titles" later in this chapter.

Printing Cell Comments

Some cells contain data or formulas that require an explanation or special attention. Comments provide a way to attach this type of information to individual cells. A red triangle in the upper-right corner of the cell indicates that a comment is present. Feel free to revisit Chapter 3, "Entering and Managing Data" for more information on comments.

This task shows you how to print your worksheets so that the printouts include the information in your comments, either as they appear in the worksheet or at the end of the worksheet.

1. Click the Page Layout tab.

2. Click the Page Setup dialog launcher.

3. On the Sheet tab, click the Comments field drop-down arrow, and choose At End of Sheet, As Displayed on Sheet, or (None).

4. Click OK.

As Displayed on Sheet

You must have your comments "showing" in your worksheet (click the Review tab and then click Show All Comments) for them to display when the As Displayed on Sheet Option is selected. If they aren't showing, they won't display in the printout or in Print Preview.

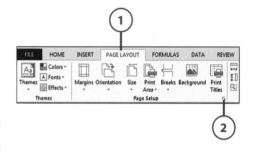

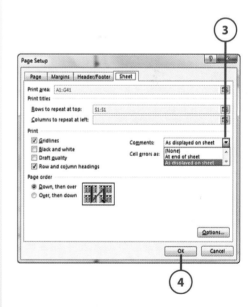

Printing Cell Error Indicators

When you print worksheets for friends or colleagues (or even yourself), calculation errors that appear on your worksheet can create a negative impression, which is why they're not printed by default. If you want these errors to be visible in your printout, however, you can display them or replace them with any of the following: <Blank>, --, or #N/A.

1. Click the Page Layout tab.

2. Click the Page Setup dialog launcher.

3. On the Sheet tab, click the drop-down arrow next to the Cell Errors As field and choose Displayed, <Blank>, --, or #N/A depending on how you want errors to be displayed.

4 Click OK.

Errors That Print

By default, Excel prints all the error messages explained in Chapter 5, "Working with Formulas and Functions," (#DIV/o!, #Name?, #Value!, #REF!, and Circular Reference errors).

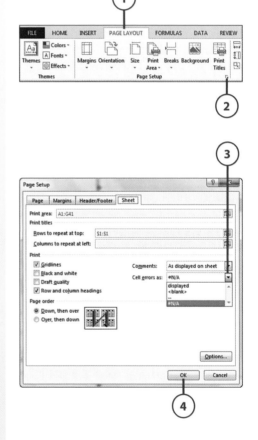

Printing Repeating Row and Column Titles

You might have noticed that when a worksheet spans multiple pages, it is difficult to keep the column and row titles organized. A quick way to rectify this is to make particular titles repeat on each page of the printed worksheet.

1. Click the Page Layout tab.

2. Click the Print Titles button.

3. Click the Rows to Repeat at Top selection box in the Print titles area.

4. Excel takes you back to your worksheet where you click the row containing the titles that you want to repeat on each page of your worksheet. Press Enter to reopen the Page Setup dialog box with your selection inserted.

5. Click OK.

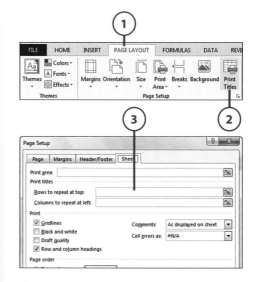

Repeating Column Headings

To repeat column headings across several pages, follow the steps in this task, but click the Columns to Repeat at the Left selection box in step 2. Then click the columns you want to repeat and proceed as normal.

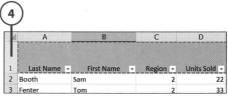

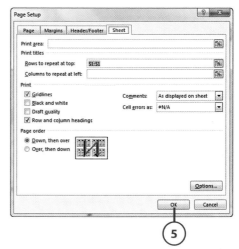

Adding Headers and Footers

Headers and footers appear at the top and bottom of printed pages of Excel worksheets and can display the filename, the date and time the worksheet was printed, and the worksheet's name, or you can create your own custom header or footer.

1. Click the Page Layout tab.

2. Click the Page Setup dialog launcher.

3. On the Header/Footer tab, click the down arrow next to the Header field, and scroll through the header options. If you see one you like, click it to see what it looks like.

4. Click the down arrow next to the Footer, and scroll through the footer options. If you see one you like, click it to see what it looks like.

5. Click OK.

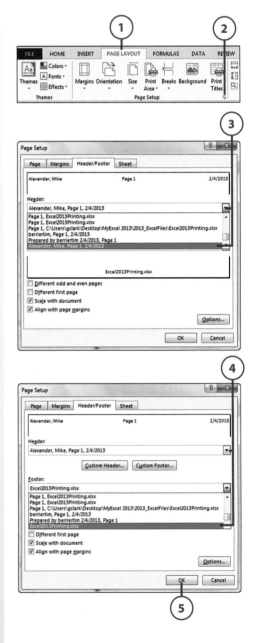

6. You can view the worksheet in Print Preview mode to get an idea of what your printed worksheet will look like with headers and footers.

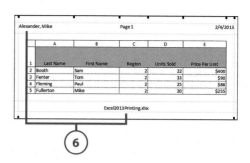

6

Easy Editing of Headers and Footers

On the View tab, you can click the Page Layout option to see your worksheet in page layout view, which enables you to see how your worksheet will look on a page. While in this view, Excel clearly shows you the header and footer for your worksheet. You can even click into the header or footer and edit them to suit your needs.

Printing Your Worksheets

Printing a worksheet, workbook, or chart sheet is quite simple, but setting the options for printing can be complex. The number of options that must be set before printing depends on the amount of data stored in the workbook, how it is arranged, how much of it needs to be printed, and how you want the printout to look.

1. With the worksheet you want to print open, click the File tab on the Ribbon.

2. Click Print.

3. Click the Printer drop-down and select the printer or fax you want to use.

4. Type the number of copies you want to print in the Number of Copies field, which defaults to 1.

5. Choose whether you want to print the Active Sheets (the currently selected sheets), the Selection (the currently selected cells), or the Entire Workbook (all worksheets and chart sheets).

6. If you want the printed pages to be collated, click the Collate drop-down to set that option.

7. Click the Print button to send your printout to the printer.

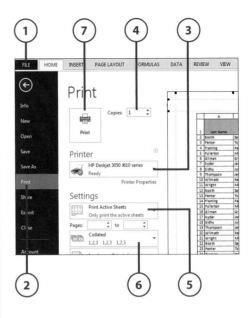

QUICK PRINTING

>>>Go Further

You can add the Quick Print command to your Quick Access toolbar. This enables you to print without going to the Backstage view. However, be aware that if you simply click the Quick Print command, your entire worksheet prints using the default printing options unless you have changed them before.

Revisit Chapter 1, "Working with Excel's Ribbon Menus," for a refresher on how to add commands to the Quick Access Toolbar.

Filters area

Columns area

Rows area

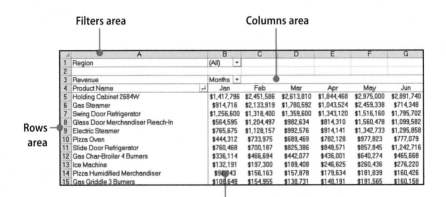

Values area

In this chapter, you discover one of Excel's best analytical tools—the Pivot Table. A pivot table is an analysis tool that enables you to create an interactive view of your data, called a pivot table report. The topics covered in this chapter include the following:

9

→ Creating a pivot table
→ Rearranging and adding a pivot table data
→ Adding a report filter
→ Refreshing pivot table data
→ Customizing field names
→ Applying numeric formats and summary calculations
→ Showing and hiding data items
→ Sorting your pivot table

Working with Pivot Tables

With a pivot table report, you can quickly and easily categorize your data into groups, summarize large amounts of data into meaningful information, and perform a variety of calculations in a fraction of the time it takes to do it by hand. The real power of a pivot table report is that you can interactively drag and drop fields within your report, dynamically changing your perspective and recalculating totals to fit your current view.

A pivot table is composed of four areas: the Values area, the Rows area, the Columns area, and the Filters area.

The Values area is the area that calculates and counts data. The Rows area displays the unique field values down the rows of the left side of the pivot table. The Columns area displays the unique field values across the top of the pivot table. The Filters area is an optional set of one or more drop-downs at the top of the pivot table.

Creating a Pivot Table

Before you create a pivot table, you should ask two questions; "What am I measuring?" and "How do I want to see it?" The answers to these questions can give you some guidance when determining in which areas to place your data fields.

The goal for the example is to show dollar sales by market, which requires a Sales field and a Market field. Markets go down the left side of the report and dollar sales are calculated next to each market.

1. Click any single cell inside your data table.

2. Click the PivotTable command on the Insert tab on the Ribbon.

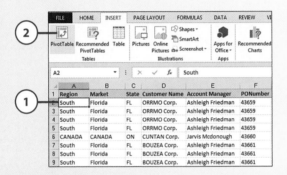

3. This activates the Create PivotTable dialog box. Specify the location of your source data and then click the OK button.

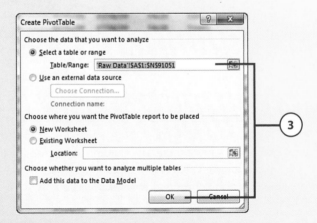

4. Observe that you have an empty pivot table report on a new worksheet. Next to the pivot table, you see the PivotTable Fields pane.

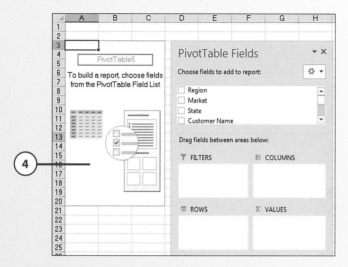

Pivot Table Default Location

In the Create PivotTable dialog box, the default location for a new pivot table is New Worksheet. This means your pivot table is placed in a new worksheet within the current workbook. You can change this by selecting the Existing Worksheet option and specifying the worksheet on which you want the pivot table to be placed.

5. Find the Market field in the field selector, and place a check next to it. The Market field is automatically placed in the Rows area of the pivot table.

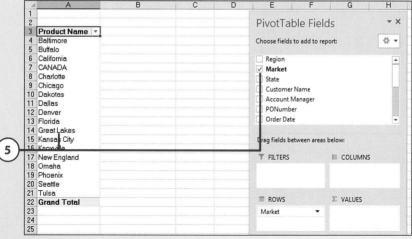

6. Scroll down the list of PivotTable fields, and find the Sale Amount field. Place a check next to it; the Sale Amount field is automatically placed in the Values area.

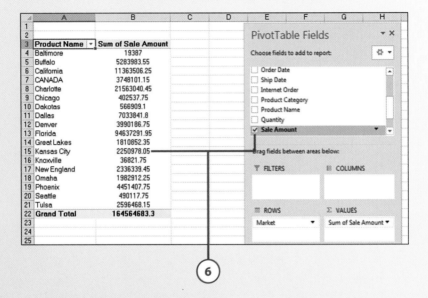

7. Click someplace other than your pivot table to make the PivotTable Fields pane disappear. Observe your first pivot table.

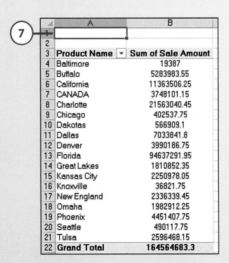

How Excel Knows Where to Place Data

Placing a check next to any field that is non-numeric (text or date) automatically places that field into the rows area of the pivot table. Placing a check next to any field that is numeric automatically places that field in the values area of the pivot table.

Activating the PivotTable Fields Pane

The PivotTable Fields pane typically activates when you click anywhere on your pivot table. If clicking the pivot table doesn't activate the PivotTable Fields pane, you can manually activate it by right-clicking anywhere inside the pivot table and selecting Show Field List.

Rearranging a Pivot Table

The nifty thing about pivot tables is that you can add as many layers of analysis as made possible by the fields in your source data table. For instance, if you want to show the dollar sales each market earned by product category, you could simply drag the Product Category field to the Columns area.

1. Click anywhere on your pivot table to reactivate the PivotTable Fields pane.

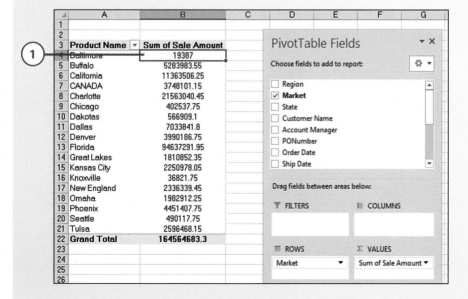

2. Find the Product Category field, click it, and drag it to the Columns area in the PivotTable Fields pane.

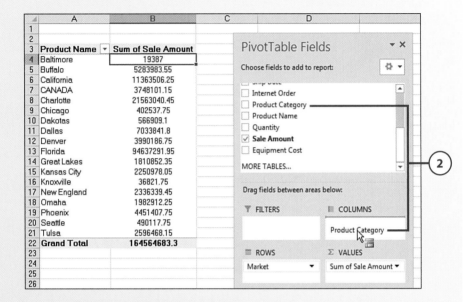

3. Click someplace other than your pivot table to make the PivotTable Fields pane disappear, and your pivot table now shows a matrix style view.

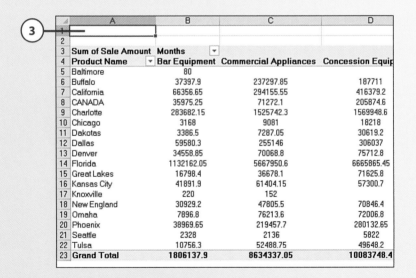

Dragging Fields from One Area to Another

You're not limited to dragging fields only from the field list. You can drag fields from one area to another. For example, you can drag the product category field from the Columns area to the Rows area. This is a fairly powerful benefit because it enables you to experiment with the look and feel of your pivot table reports.

Adding a Report Filter

Often, you're asked to produce reports for one particular region, market, product, and so on. Instead of working hours and hours building separate reports for every possible analysis scenario, you can leverage pivot tables to help create multiple views of the same data. For example, you can do so by creating a region filter in your pivot table.

1. Click anywhere on your pivot table to reactivate the PivotTable Fields pane.

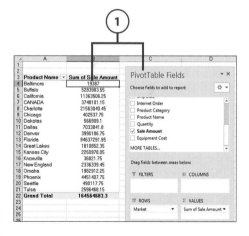

2. Find the Region field, click it, and drag it to the Filters area in the PivotTable Fields pane.

3. Your pivot table now has a filter drop-down for Region.

Using a Field's Context Menu to Move It

In addition to dragging, you can also move a field into the different areas of the pivot table by clicking the black triangle next to the field name and then selecting the wanted area.

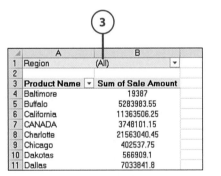

4. After you have a report filter on your pivot table, you can click the filters drop-down and select the wanted data item.

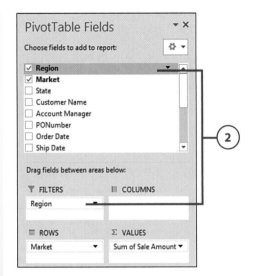

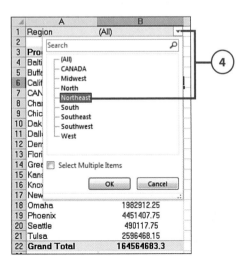

5. Now the pivot table responds by showing you only the data for the selected item.

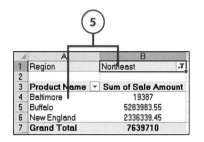

Selecting Multiple Data Items

When you click the filters drop-down to select a data item, you can see the check box labeled Select Multiple Items. Clicking this check box enables you to select more than one data item to filter your report by.

Refreshing Pivot Table Data

When you create a pivot table, Excel takes a snapshot of your data source and stores it in a pivot cache. A pivot cache is a special memory container. This is what your pivot table connects to. That's right; your pivot table report is essentially a view that gets its data solely from the pivot cache. This means that your pivot table report and your data source are disconnected.

The benefit of working against the pivot cache and not your original data source is optimization. Any changes you make to the pivot table report, such as rearranging fields, adding new fields, or hiding items, are made rapidly and with minimal overhead.

However, because your pivot table works from a snapshot of your data source, any changes you make to your data are not picked up by your pivot table report until you take another snapshot. This is called "refreshing" your pivot table.

1. Right-click anywhere in your pivot table.

2. Select the Refresh option.

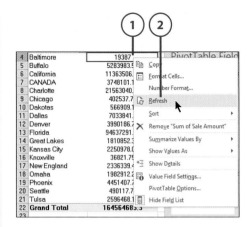

The PivotTable Tools Contextual Tab

When you click your pivot table, Excel activates the PivotTable Tools contextual tabs. There, you see an Analyze tab and a Design tab. Click the Analyze tab and choose the Refresh command. These tabs expose a variety of commands you can use to manage and work with pivot tables.

Adding Pivot Table Data

Sometimes, the data source that feeds your pivot table changes in structure. For example, you might have added or deleted rows or columns from your data table. These types of changes affect the range of your data source, not just a few data items in the table. In these cases, performing a simple Refresh of your pivot table won't do. You must update the range being captured by the pivot table.

1. Click anywhere in your pivot table to activate the PivotTable Tools contextual tabs.

2. Select the Change Data Source command in the Analyze tab.

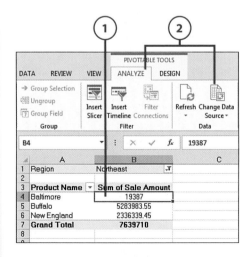

3. The Change PivotTable Data Source dialog box activates. Supply the new data range for the pivot table in this box.

4. Click OK to confirm the change. Your pivot table automatically refreshes to show the newly referenced data.

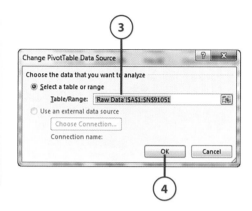

CHANGING THE PIVOT TABLE LAYOUT

Excel 2013 gives you a choice of three layouts for your pivot tables. The three layouts are the Compact form, Outline form, and Tabular form. Although no layout stands out as being better than the others, the most popular layout is, by far, the Tabular form. This is mainly because the tabular layout was the one that existed in previous versions of Excel, so most people who have seen pivot tables in the past are used to that layout. Choose the pivot table format by clicking inside your pivot table, clicking the Report the Layout drop-down on the Design tab, and then selecting the appropriate pivot table style.

Row Labels	Sales
⊟Australia	1622869.422
Accessories	23973.9186
Bikes	1351872.837
Clothing	43231.6124
Components	203791.0536
⊟Canada	14463280.15
Accessories	119302.5429
Bikes	11714700.47
Clothing	383021.7229
Components	2246255.419
⊟Central	7932851.609
Accessories	46551.211
Bikes	6782978.335
Clothing	155873.9547
Components	947448.1091
⊟France	4647454.207
Accessories	48941.5643
Bikes	3597879.394
Clothing	129508.0548
Components	871125.1938
⊟Germany	2051547.729
Accessories	35681.4552
Bikes	1602487.163
Clothing	75592.5945
Components	337786.516

Compact form layout

Market	Segment	Sales
⊟Australia		1622869.422
	Accessories	23973.9186
	Bikes	1351872.837
	Clothing	43231.6124
	Components	203791.0536
⊟Canada		14463280.15
	Accessories	119302.5429
	Bikes	11714700.47
	Clothing	383021.7229
	Components	2246255.419
⊟Central		7932851.609
	Accessories	46551.211
	Bikes	6782978.335
	Clothing	155873.9547
	Components	947448.1091
⊟France		4647454.207
	Accessories	48941.5643
	Bikes	3597879.394
	Clothing	129508.0548
	Components	871125.1938
⊟Germany		2051547.729
	Accessories	35681.4552
	Bikes	1602487.163
	Clothing	75592.5945
	Components	337786.516

Outline form layout

Market	Segment	Sales
⊟Australia	Accessories	23973.9186
	Bikes	1351872.837
	Clothing	43231.6124
	Components	203791.0536
Australia Total		1622869.422
⊟Canada	Accessories	119302.5429
	Bikes	11714700.47
	Clothing	383021.7229
	Components	2246255.419
Canada Total		14463280.15
⊟Central	Accessories	46551.211
	Bikes	6782978.335
	Clothing	155873.9547
	Components	947448.1091
Central Total		7932851.609
⊟France	Accessories	48941.5643
	Bikes	3597879.394
	Clothing	129508.0548
	Components	871125.1938
France Total		4647454.207
⊟Germany	Accessories	35681.4552
	Bikes	1602487.163
	Clothing	75592.5945
	Components	337786.516
Germany Total		2051547.729

Tabular form layout

Customizing Field Names

Every field in your pivot table has a name. The fields in the rows, columns, and filters areas inherit their names from the data labels in your source table. The fields in the Values area are given a name, such as Sum of Sale Amount. Often you might prefer another name for your fields. For instance, you might want your Value field called Total Sales instead of Sum of Sale Amount.

1. Right-click the field Sum of Sale Amount.

2. Select Value Field Settings.

3. Enter the new name in the Custom Name input box, and click OK to confirm.

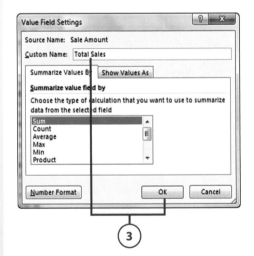

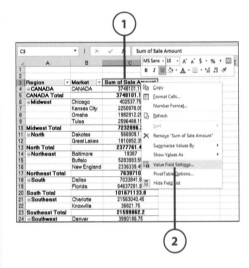

4. Note that the name of your pivot field changed.

	A	B	C
1			
2			
3	Region ▼	Market ▼	Total Sales
4	⊟CANADA	CANADA	3748101.15
5	CANADA Total		3748101.15
6	⊟Midwest	Chicago	402537.75
7		Kansas City	2250978.05
8		Omaha	1982912.25
9		Tulsa	2596468.15
10	Midwest Total		7232896.2
11	⊟North	Dakotas	566909.1
12		Great Lakes	1810852.35
13	North Total		2377761.45

Pivot Field Naming Restriction

You cannot rename a pivot field to the same name used in your source table. For example, if you try to rename Sum of Sale Amount as Sale Amount, you get an error message because there's already a Sale Amount field in the source data table.

To get around this, you can name the field and add a space to the end of the name. Excel considers Sale Amount (followed by a space) to be different from Sale Amount. This way you can use the name you want, and no one will notice it's any different.

Applying Numeric Formats to Data Fields

You can format numbers in pivot tables to fit your needs (that is, you can format them as currency, percentage, or number). You can easily control the numeric formatting of a field using the Value Field Settings dialog box.

1. Right-click any value within the target field. For example, if you want to change the format of the values in the Total Sales field, right-click any value under that field.

2. Select Value Field Settings.

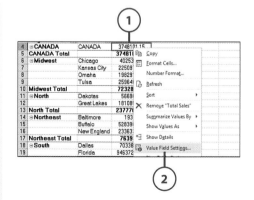

3. Click the Number Format button in the Value Field Settings dialog box.

4. Use the Format Cells dialog box to apply the number format you want, just as you normally would on your spreadsheet. Click OK.

5. After you set the formatting for a field, the applied formatting persists even if you refresh or rearrange your pivot table.

Getting to Field Settings from the Ribbon

You can also get to the Value Field Settings dialog box via the Ribbon. Simply click the Field Settings command on the Analyze tab.

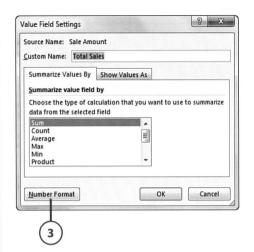

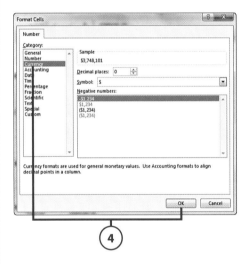

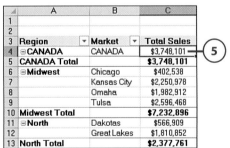

Changing Summary Calculations

When creating your pivot table report, Excel, by default, summarizes your data by either counting or summing the items. Instead of Sum or Count, you might want to choose functions, such as Average, Min, Max, and so on. You can easily change the summary calculation for any given field by taking the following actions:

1. Right-click any value within the target field.

2. Select Value Field Settings.

3. Choose the type of calculation you want to use from the list of calculations in the Value Field Settings, and then click OK to confirm.

4. Note that the pivot table now shows your chosen calculation.

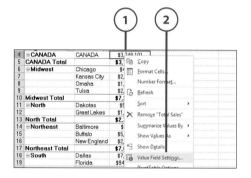

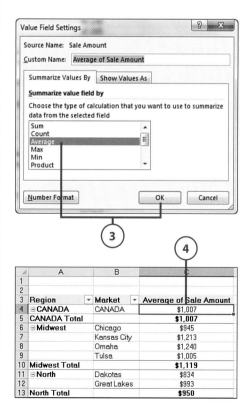

It's Not All Good

How Excel Chooses Sum or Count

When you click a numeric field in the PivotTable Fields pane, Excel automatically places that field in the Values area. However, Excel doesn't necessarily apply a Sum to that field.

If all the cells in a column contain numeric data, Excel chooses a Sum calculation by default. However, if just one cell in that same column is either blank or contains text, Excel chooses the Count calculation.

Be sure to pay attention to the fields that you place into the values area of the pivot table. If the field name starts with Count Of, Excel counts the items in the field instead of summing the values.

Showing and Hiding Data Items

A pivot table summarizes and displays all the records in your source data table. However, there might be situations in which you want to inhibit certain data items from being included in your pivot table summary. In these situations, you can choose to hide a data item. In terms of pivot tables, hiding doesn't just mean preventing the data item from being shown on the report, but hiding a data item also prevents it from being factored into the summary calculations. For example, you can hide the Canada market to see only sales for U.S. markets.

1. Click the drop-down for the field you are filtering, in this case, the Market field.

2. Remove the check from the data item you want hidden. In the example, Canada is being removed so that only U.S. sales are calculated. Click OK.

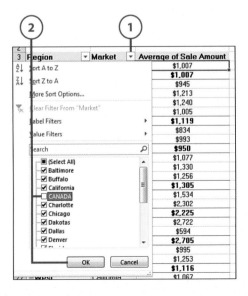

3. After the filter has been applied, the Canada market is hidden, and the grand total has recalculated to show the total of U.S. markets only.

	A	B	C
1			
2			
3	**Region** ▾	**Market** ▾	**Total Sales**
4	⊟ Midwest	Chicago	$402,538
5		Kansas City	$2,250,978
6		Omaha	$1,982,912
7		Tulsa	$2,596,468
8	**Midwest Total**		**$7,232,896**
9	⊟ North	Dakotas	$566,909
10		Great Lakes	$1,810,852
11	**North Total**		**$2,377,761**
12	⊟ Northeast	Baltimore	$19,387
13		Buffalo	$5,283,984
14		New England	$2,336,339
15	**Northeast Total**		**$7,639,710**
16	⊟ South	Dallas	$7,033,842
17		Florida	$94,637,292
18	**South Total**		**$101,671,134**
19	⊟ Southeast	Charlotte	$21,563,040
20		Knoxville	$36,822
21	**Southeast Total**		**$21,599,862**
22	⊟ Southwest	Denver	$3,990,187
23		Phoenix	$4,451,408
24	**Southwest Total**		**$8,441,595**
25	⊟ West	California	$11,363,506
26		Seattle	$490,118
27	**West Total**		**$11,853,624**
28	**Grand Total**		**$160,816,582**

(3)

Clear Applied Filters

To return a pivot field to its normal unfiltered state, right-click any value for that field, and select Filter, Clear Filter from *field name* (where *field name* is the name of the field you're working with). To clear all the filters in the pivot table at one time, go to the Analyze tab, click the Clear command, and then click Clear All.

Sorting Your Pivot Table

By default, items in each pivot field are sorted in ascending sequence based on the item name. Excel gives you the freedom to change the sort order of the items in your pivot table. Like many actions you can perform in Excel, there are dozens of different ways to sort data within a pivot table. The easiest way is to apply the sort directly in the pivot table.

1. Right-click any value within the target field.

2. Select Sort.

3. Select your sort direction. In the example, the data is sorted on Total Sales with the largest numbers at the top.

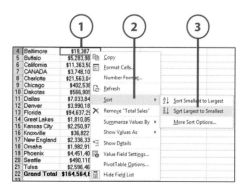

4. Note that the pivot table now sorts the values per your instructions.

	A	B
1		
2		
3	**Market** ↴	**Total Sales**
4	Florida	$94,637,292
5	Charlotte	$21,563,040
6	California	$11,363,506
7	Dallas	$7,033,842
8	Buffalo	$5,283,984
9	Phoenix	$4,451,408
10	Denver	$3,990,187
11	CANADA	$3,748,101
12	Tulsa	$2,596,468
13	New England	$2,336,339
14	Kansas City	$2,250,978
15	Omaha	$1,982,912
16	Great Lakes	$1,810,852
17	Dakotas	$566,909
18	Seattle	$490,118
19	Chicago	$402,538
20	Knoxville	$36,822
21	Baltimore	$19,387
22	**Grand Total**	**$164,564,683**

Sorting Persists in a Pivot Table

When you sort data in a standard worksheet, it's actually a one-time event. Therefore, if you add data to your data table after sorting, you need to sort again. In a pivot table, however, the sorting persists. If new data is introduced to a sorted pivot table, the new value is automatically sorted and based on the sort rules you implement. You do not need to reapply the sort.

An Excel Workbook Opened in a Web Browser via SkyDrive

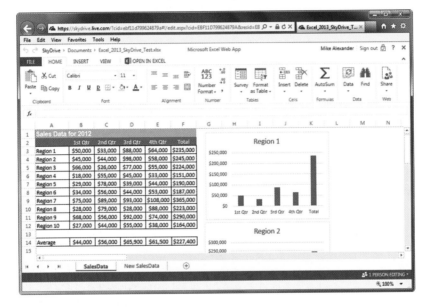

In this chapter, you find out how to leverage SkyDrive to store and share Excel files on the Internet. The topics covered in this chapter include the following:

→ Signing up for SkyDrive
→ Signing into SkyDrive
→ Saving a workbook to SkyDrive
→ Opening a SkyDrive workbook
→ Downloading a workbook from SkyDrive
→ Sharing a SkyDrive workbook with others
→ Managing SkyDrive workbooks

Using SkyDrive to Store and Share Excel Files

You can think of SkyDrive as a Microsoft Office platform in the cloud (or as Microsoft's answer to Google Spreadsheets). With it you can save, view, and edit your Office documents on the Web. When you publish your Excel workbooks to SkyDrive, you can

- View and edit your workbooks from any browser, even if the computer you use doesn't have Excel installed.

- Provide a platform in which two or more people can collaborate on and edit the same Excel file at the same time.

- Share workbooks with others by via web links.

Signing Up For SkyDrive

Before you can use SkyDrive, you need to sign up for a Microsoft passport account. Follow these steps to create an account.

1. Open your web browser and enter skydrive.live.com in the address bar.

2. Click the Sign Up Now link.

3. Complete the registration form to create your account.

Hotmail Users Can Skip This Step

If you have a Hotmail email account, you already have an account with Microsoft. You can use your Hotmail email address and password to sign into SkyDrive.

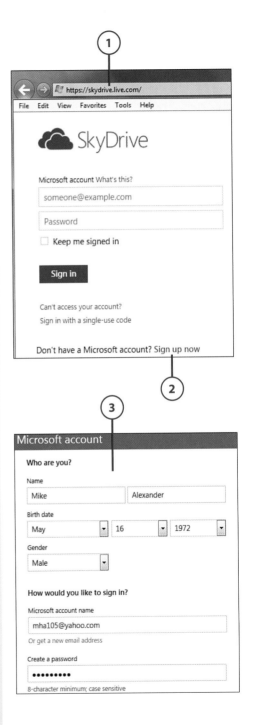

Signing into SkyDrive

After you have a SkyDrive account, you need to sign into your SkyDrive account. Signing in through Excel automatically ties your SkyDrive account to any Excel document you open.

1. Open any Excel document and click the File tab.

2. Click the Save As button.

3. Click SkyDrive.

4. Click the Sign In button.

5. Enter the email address you used to register for your Microsoft account.

6. Click the Sign In button.

7. Enter the password you created when registering for your Microsoft account.

8. Click the Sign In button.

9. Note your SkyDrive account in the Save As pane.

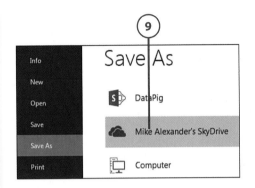

You Only Have to Sign In Once

After signing in one time, Microsoft Office remembers your SkyDrive credentials and automatically signs in for you each time you open an Office document. Your SkyDrive account appears in the Backstage view of any Microsoft Office document you open.

Saving a Workbook to SkyDrive

When you save a workbook to SkyDrive, you are essentially publishing your Excel workbook to the Web. You have a good bit of control over which components of your Excel workbook are viewable on the Web through Excel's Browser View options described here.

1. Open the workbook you want published to SkyDrive, and click the File tab.

2. Click the Save As button.

3. Double-click your SkyDrive Account.

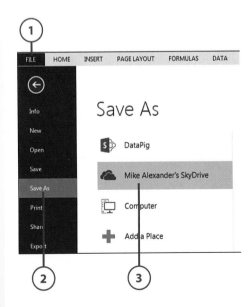

4. Click the Documents folder in the Save As dialog box.

5. Click the Browser View Options button.

Creating a New Folder

By default, SkyDrive starts you with a folder called Documents. This folder is a fine location to save your workbooks. However, if you need to create a separate folder for your workbook, click the New Folder option in the Save As dialog box.

6. Click the drop-down and select Sheets.

7. Place a check next to each sheet you want to make available on the Web. Remove the check next to any sheet you don't want to share.

8. Click the OK button to return to the Save As dialog box.

9. Click the Save button to publish your workbook.

Saving Certain Objects in the Workbook

In addition to Sheets, the drop-down shown in step 6 has an option called Items in the Workbook. When this option is selected, you can choose to show or not show certain objects in the workbook. For instance, you might have four charts in the workbook but want to make only two of them visible on the Web. Simply uncheck the charts you don't want published. You can control the visibility of any object inserted in your workbook—charts, shapes, pictures, pivot tables, and so on.

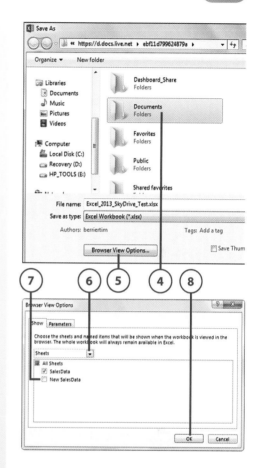

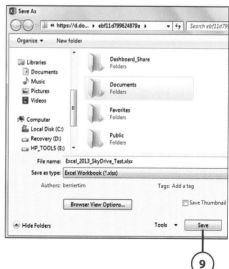

Opening a SkyDrive Workbook

After you publish your workbook to SkyDrive, you can open, view, and edit it through any browser. This enables access to your workbook from any computer, even if that computer doesn't have Microsoft Excel installed on it. And because your workbook is on the Web, any number of people can open and edit your workbook, allowing for easy collaboration. Follow these steps to open a workbook on SkyDrive.

1. Open your browser, enter skydrive.live.com in the address bar, and sign into your SkyDrive account.

2. Click Files.

3. Double-click the folder in which you saved your workbook.

4. Double-click the file you want to view or edit.

5. Your workbook opens directly in the browser, enabling you to work with it just as you would if it were opened in Excel.

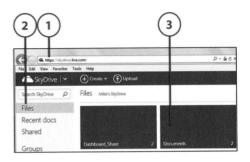

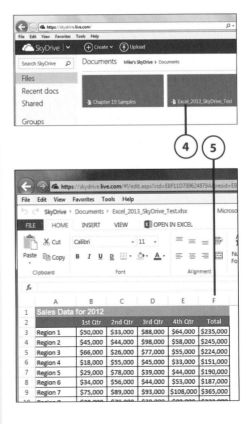

It's Not All Good

Workbooks on SkyDrive Have Limitations

Workbooks that run on the Web run in an Excel Web App that is quite different from the Excel client application you have on your PC. The Excel Web App has limitations on the features it can render in the web browser. Some limitations exist due to security issues, whereas others exist simply because Microsoft hasn't had time to evolve the Excel Web App to include the broad set of features that come with standard Excel.

In any case, the following is a list of some of the limitations of the Excel Web App as of this writing:

- Data Validation does not work on the Web. This feature is simply ignored when you publish your workbook to the Web.

- No form of VBA code (including macros), run in the Excel Web App.

- Worksheet protection does not work on the Web.

- Links to external workbooks no longer work after you publish to the Web.

- You can use any pivot tables with full fidelity on the Web, but you cannot create any new pivot tables while your workbook is on the Web. You need to create any pivot tables in the Excel client on your PC before publishing on the Web.

Downloading a Workbook from SkyDrive

You might find that you want to download a copy of a SkyDrive workbook to your local PC. In these cases, you can follow the steps outlined here.

1. With your SkyDrive workbook open, click the File tab.

2. Click the Save As button.

3. Click the Download button.

4. Use the Save As dialog box to specify the location and name of the file and then click the Save button.

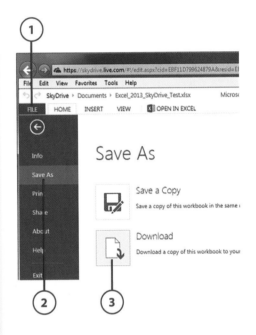

Sharing Your SkyDrive Workbooks with Others

One of the major benefits of publishing your workbooks to SkyDrive is that multiple people can view and edit your Excel files simply by going to the appropriate web link. Excel makes it easy for you to distribute these web links through the Share feature of SkyDrive.

1. With your SkyDrive workbook open, click the File tab.

2. Click the Share button.

3. Click the Share with People button.

4. Click the Send Email option.

5. Enter the appropriate email address.

6. Enter some text for the body of the email.

7. Choose whether you want the recipients of your link to have rights to edit the workbook and whether you require them to log in to see the workbook.

8. Click the Share button to send the email.

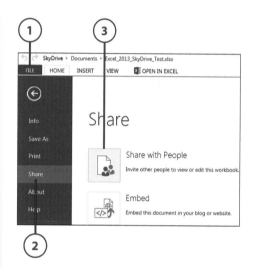

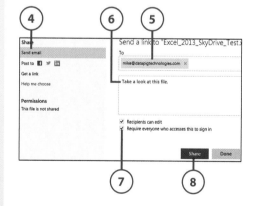

Sending to multiple recipients

To send to multiple email addresses, simply separate the email addresses with a semicolon (;).

Managing SkyDrive Workbooks

After your workbooks are in a SkyDrive folder, you may want to do things such as delete them, rename them, copy them, and move them around. Follow these steps to perform these sorts of actions on your SkyDrive workbooks.

1. Open your browser, enter skydrive.live.com into the address bar and sign in to your SkyDrive account.

2. Click Files.

3. Double-click the folder that contains your target workbook.

4. Place a check in the check box of the target workbook and then right-click the box to open the pop-up menu.

5. Choose the wanted action.

Taking Actions on Multiple Workbooks

You can take actions on multiple workbooks at once by first placing a check in all the targeted workbooks and then right-clicking any one of them. When you select multiple workbooks, your actions are limited to Download, Delete, and Move To.

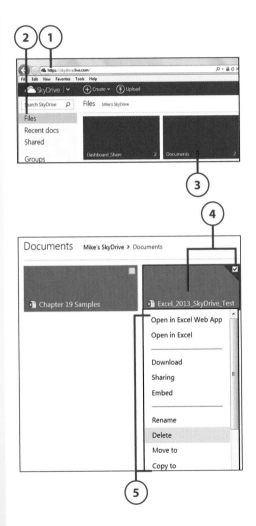

Recovering Deleted Files in SkyDrive

When you delete a file in SkyDrive, it is sent to a recycle bin folder in SkyDrive. That recycle bin can be used to recover deleted files just as you would in your standard operating system. But be aware that when the recycle bin starts taking up more than 10% of your storage limit, SkyDrive starts deleting your older content and also permanently deletes files that were in the bin for more than 30 days.

Excel Shortcut Keys

Excel shortcut keys enable you to perform certain tasks using only the keyboard. The idea is that you increase your efficiency when you limit the number of instances your hands have to move back and forth from the keyboard to the mouse. Not only that, but it's often quicker (requires fewer steps) to perform tasks using simple keystrokes rather than using the mouse. Getting in the habit of using these shortcut keys can help you work more efficiently and become more productive.

Using the Excel Shortcut Key Reference Table

Table A.1 lists the keyboard shortcuts you can use as an ongoing reference of the more commonly used Excel shortcut keys.

The Key column tells which root key on the keyboard you press. The Alone column tells you what task is triggered if you press the root key by itself. Some keys (such as the F1 key) trigger a task when you press them alone, whereas others (such as the letter A) do not perform a task.

The Shift column tells you what task is triggered if you press the root key and the Shift key. For example, when you press the F5 key with the Shift key (Shift+F5) the Find dialog box activates.

The Ctrl column tells you what task is triggered if you press the root key with the Ctrl key. For example, when you press the B key with the Ctrl key (Ctrl+B) bold is applied to the selected text.

The Alt column tells you what task is triggered if you press the root key with the Alt key. For example, when you press the F4 key with the Alt key (Alt+F4) Excel closes.

The Ctrl+Shift column tells you what task is triggered if you press the root key with the Ctrl and the Shift keys. For example, when you press the F12 key with the Ctrl and Shift keys (Ctrl+Shift+F12) the active workbook prints.

Table A.1   Excel Shortcut Keys

Key	Alone	Shift	Ctrl	Alt	Ctrl+Shift
F1	Help	What's This Help	Displays or hides the Ribbon	Insert Chart Sheet	
F2	Edit Mode	Add or Edit Comment	Displays Print Preview Area	Save As	
F3	Paste Name	InsertFunction	Define Name		Names from Labels
F4	Repeat Action	Find Again	Close Window	Quit Excel	
F5	Go To	Find	Restore Window Size		
F6	Next Pane	Prev Pane	Next Workbook	Switch to VBA	Prev Workbook
F7	Spell Check		Move Window		
F8	Extend Selection	Add to Selection	Resize Window	Macro List	
F9	Calculate All	Calculate Worksheet	Minimize Workbook		
F10	Activate Menu	Context Menu	Restore Workbook		
F11	New Chart	New Worksheet	New Macro Sheet	VB Editor	
F12	Save As	Save	Open		Print
A			Select All		

Key	Alone	Shift	Ctrl	Alt	Ctrl+Shift
B			Bold		
C			Copy		
D			Fill Down		
F			Find		Font
G			Go To		
H			Replace		
I			Italic		
K			Insert Hyperlink		
N			New Workbook		
O			Open Workbook		Select Comments
P			Print		Font
Q			Quick Analysis		
R			Fill Right		
S			Save		
T			Create Table	Tools Menu	
U			Underline		Expand/Collapse Formula bar
V			Paste		Paste Special
W			Close Workbook	Window Menu	
X			Cut		
Y			Repeat Action		
Z			Undo		
~					General Format
!					Number Format
@					Time Format
#					Date Format
$					Currency Format
%					Percent Format
^					Scientific Format

Key	Alone	Shift	Ctrl	Alt	Ctrl+Shift
*					Select Region
(					Unhide Rows
)					Unhide Columns
-				Control Menu	No Border
+	Formula			Auto Sum	Insert Dialog
;			Insert Date	Select Visible Cells	
'				Style	Copy Cell Value Above
:					Insert Time
/			Select Array		Select Array
\			Select Differences		Select Unequal Cells
Insert	Insert Mode		Copy		
Delete	Clear		Delete to End of Line		
Home	Begin Row		Start of Worksheet		
End	End Row		End of Worksheet		
Page Up	Page Up		Previous Worksheet	Left 1 screen	
Page Down	Page Down		Next Worksheet	Right 1 Screen	Select Down
Left Arrow	Move Left	Select Left	Move Left Area		Select Left
Right Arrow	Move Right	Select Right	Move Right Area		Select Right
Up Arrow	Move Up	Select Up	Move Up Area		Select Up
Down Arrow	Move Down	Select Down	Move Down Area	Drop Down List	Select Down
Space Bar	Space	Select Row	Select Column	Control Box	Select Entire Used Range
Tab	Move Right	Move Left	Next Window	Next Application	Previous Window

Index

Symbols

#DIV/0! error, troubleshooting, 119-120

error, troubleshooting, 59

#NAME? error, troubleshooting, 120-122

#REF! error, troubleshooting, 124-126

#VALUE! error, troubleshooting, 122-123

A

Accounting format, 62

activating Fields pane (pivot tables), 199

active chart element, displaying, 144

adding
  cell comments, 50-51
  commands to Quick Access Toolbar, 10-12
  data to charts, 149-150
  footers, 190-191
  groups to Quick Access Toolbar, 12
  headers, 190-191
  hidden commands to Quick Access Toolbar, 13
  legends to charts, 150
  pivot table data, 204-205
  Quick Print command to Quick Access toolbar, 192
  report filter to pivot tables, 201-203
  WordArt, 160

adjusting page margins, 177-178

Align Left command, 68

alignment
  changing, 70
  of chart axes, changing, 147
  of wrapped text, 72

Alt+Tab toggle, switching between open workbooks, 19

angle of cell orientation, changing, 71

applying
  bold formatting, 65-66
  cell references from other worksheets, 101-104
  conditional formatting, 85
  custom formatting styles, 84-85
  data filters, 48
  italic formatting, 65-68
  styles to shapes, 154

arguments
  entering for
    functions, 107
  Type argument, 110
Arrange All command, 20
arranging workbooks,
  20-22
assigning names to
  ranges, 99
Auto-Calculate feature,
  104-105
AutoShapes, 154, 158-159
  formatting, 159
  moving, 159
  resizing, 159
AutoSum calculations,
  89-94
  resultant cells, 90
  shortcut key, 90-131
AVERAGE function, 91
axes (charts)
  alignment,
    changing, 147
  gridlines, formatting,
    146-147
  scale, formatting,
    146-147

B

background color
  of cells, changing, 57
  of chart area,
    changing, 145
  of charts, changing, 138
  of plot area,
    changing, 143
Backstage view, 6, 15
  printing options, 173
  workbooks, closing, 17
bold formatting, applying,
  65-66
borders
  changing, 72-73
  removing, 73

buttons
  Chart Elements, 138
  Close, 17
  Online Pictures, 156-171
  Page Break Preview, 174
  Picture, 157-171

C

calculating
  cell average with
    AVERAGE function, 91
  future value of invest-
    ments with FV func-
    tion, 115-117
  largest cell amount with
    MAX function, 92
  loan payments with
    PMT function, 107-110
  smallest cell amount
    with MIN function, 93
cell references, applying
  from other worksheets,
  101-104
cells, 7, 9
  background color,
    changing, 57
  borders
    changing, 74-75
    removing, 75
  column width,
    changing, 55-56
  comments
    adding, 48-51
    displaying, 51
    editing, 51
    printing, 188
  counting, 94
  dependents, 130-131
  entries, indenting, 73-74
  error indicators,
    printing, 188
  formatting, 55, 81-82
  formulas, entering, 95-96
  orientation,
    changing, 71
  overwriting, 123

precedents, 128-131
ranges
  conditional sums,
    113-115
  names, assigning, 99
  names, deleting, 101
  resultant cells, 90
  row height,
    changing, 69
  selecting for
    calculation, 91
  text color, changing, 57
  unmerging, 67
  wrapping data in, 72
centering worksheets on a
  page, 185
changing
  cells
    background color, 57
    borders, 72-73
    text color, 57
  charts, background
    color, 138
  column width, 55-56
  size of fonts, 54-55
  source data range of
    charts, 137
chart area
  background color,
    changing, 145
  formatting, 144-146
Chart Elements button, 138
charts. See also pivot tables
  active chart element,
    displaying, 144
  axes
    alignment,
      changing, 147
    number formatting,
      customizing, 139
    scale, formatting,
      146-147
  background color,
    changing, 138
  chart area
    background color,
      changing, 145
    formatting, 144-146

creating, 134-136
customizing, 142-151
data
    adding, 149-150
    excluding, 150
data labels, 140-152
data table, customizing, 141-151
formatting with Home tab commands, 146
incorrect source data, locating, 137
legends
    adding, 150
    formatting, 151
moving, 136
plot area
    background color, changing, 144
    formatting, 142-144
printing, 142-151
source data
    range of,
        changing, 137
    updating, 147-149
type of, changing, 136
Chart Tools contextual tab, 133
circular references, trouble-shooting, 126-127
Clear Contents command, 78
clearing
    formatting, 74-76
    pivot tables filter, 211
    print area, 176-192
clip art, inserting, 156-157
clip art. *See also* graphics, 157
Close button, 17
closing workbooks, 17
color, applying
    to shapes, 154
    to cell background, 57
    to cell text, 57
    to worksheet tabs, 23

columns, 8
    deleting, 43-44
    freezing, 38
    headers
        adding, 190-191
        editing, 191-192
        printing, 186
        repeating, 189
    hiding/unhiding, 44, 78-80
    inserting, 43-44
    references, 7-8
    repeating titles, printing, 189
    width of
        changing, 55-56
        fitting to content, 56
Columns area (pivot tables), 195
commands
    adding to Quick Access Toolbar, 10-13
    Align Left, 68
    Arrange All, 20
    Clear Contents, 76
    Comma Style, 58
    Increase Decimal, 58
    Insert Function, 105-117
    Merge and Center, 66-67
    Percent Style, 59
    Print Area, 176-192
    Quick Print command, adding to Quick Access toolbar, 192
    removing from Quick Access Toolbar, 13
commas, adding to numeric data, 58-87
Comma Style command, 58
comments
    adding to cells, 50-51
    editing, 51
Compact form layout (pivot tables), 205
conditional formatting, applying, 85

contextual tabs, 9, 10
    Chart tools, 133
    Format, 10
    PivotTable Tools, 204
controlling visibility of workbook objects with SkyDrive, 221
converting numeric data
    to text, 64
    to percentages, 59
copying
    data, 36-37
    formatting, 82-83
    formulas, 97-98
    objects, 169
    versus moving, 26
    worksheets between workbooks, 25-26
correcting typing mistakes, 32-33
COUNTA function, 94
COUNT function, 94
COUNTIF function, 115
counting number of cells, 94
creating
    charts, 134-136
    custom formatting styles, 84-85
    new folders in SkyDrive, 219
    pivot tables, 196-199
    workbooks, 16
Currency format, 62
customizing
    charts, 142-151
        data table, 141-151
        number
            formatting, 139
    pivot tables, field names, 206-207
    styles, 84-85
cutting and pasting data, 37
cycling through Print Preview pages, 174

D

dashes, print area, 176-192

data

error, trouble-
shooting, 59

adding to charts,
149-150

adding to pivot tables,
204-205

cell comments,
printing, 187

copying and pasting,
36-37

editing, 33

entering, 32

excluding from
charts, 150

finding, 46

formatting, clearing,
74-76

grouping with Merge
and Center command,
66-87

horizontal alignment,
changing, 68-69

moving, 44-45

numeric data

*Accounting
format, 62*

commas, adding, 58

*converting to percent-
ages, 59*

Currency format, 62

Date format, 63

formatting, 58-64

General format, 60

Number format, 61

Time format, 64

pivot tables

hiding, 210-211

sorting, 211-213

replacing, 47

sorting, 49-50

vertical alignment,
changing, 70

wrapping in a cell, 72

data filters, applying, 48

data labels, charts, 140-151

data table (charts),
customizing, 141-151

Data tab (Ribbon), 5

Date format, 63

decimal places, increasing/
decreasing in numeric
data, 61

decreasing decimal places
in numeric data, 61

default location for pivot
tables, 197

deleted files, recovering in
SkyDrive, 225

deleting

columns, 43-44

drawing objects, 155

objects, 171

range names, 101

rows, 42-43

worksheets from
workbooks, 22

deletions, undoing, 171

dependents, 130-131

diagrams

formatting with Layouts
gallery, 164

inserting, 163-164

dialog boxes

Find and Replace, 47

Open, 16

dialog launchers, 4

disabling Auto-Calculate
feature, 105

displaying

active chart
element, 144

cell comments, 51, 187

cell error indicators, 188

print area with Page
Break Preview view,
181-182

Print Preview, 174

downloading workbooks
from SkyDrive, 222

dragging pivot table fields
to other areas, 201

drawing objects

deleting, 155

modifying, 155

drawing tools, 153-155

E

editing

comments, 51

data, 33

footers, 191-192

formulas, 96-97

functions, 96-97

headers, 191-192

email

Hotmail, signing into
SkyDrive, 216

multiple recipients,
sending to, 223

workbooks, sharing, 223

embedded IF
statements, 111

entering

data, 32

formulas, 95-96

function
arguments, 107

error indicators (cells),
printing, 188

errors

error, trouble-
shooting, 59

#DIV/0! error, trouble-
shooting, 119-120

#NAME? error, trouble-
shooting, 122-123

#REF! error, trouble-
shooting, 124-126

#VALUE! error, trouble-
shooting, 122-123

troubleshooting, 118

Excel Web App, limitations
of, 221

excluding, data from
charts, 150

F

Fields pane (pivot tables),
activating, 199
fields (pivot tables)
dragging to other
areas, 201
names, customizing,
206-207
files, recovering from
SkyDrive, 225
File tab (Ribbon), 6
filters, applying, 48
Filters area (pivot
tables), 195
Find and Replace dialog
box, 47
finding
data, 46
name of fonts, 54
fitting
columns to content, 56
rows to content, 69
folders, creating in
SkyDrive, 219
fonts
changing, 54-55
names of, finding, 54-87
size of, changing, 54-55
footers
adding, 190-191
editing, 191-192
Format as Table feature,
81-82
Format contextual tabs, 10
Format dialog box,
opening, 168-171
Format Painter
copying formatting,
82-83
persistent mode,
enabling, 83
formatting
AutoShapes, 159
axes, gridlines, 139

cells, 55
chart area, 144-146
charts
axis scale, 146-147
legends, 151
plot area, 142-144
with Home tab
commands, 146
clearing, 74-76
copying, 82-83
custom styles, applying,
84-85
diagrams with Layouts
gallery, 164
Format as Table feature,
81-82
horizontal alignment,
changing, 68-69
numeric data
Date format, 63
General format, 62
Number format, 61
Text format, 64
Time format, 64
objects, 167-168
pivot tables, applying
numeric format,
207-208
text with WordArt, 160
underlining, 65-87
formulas, 89
AutoSum calculations,
89-94
copying, 97-98
dependents, 130-131
editing, 96-97
entering, 95-96
order of operation, 96
precedents, 128-131
references, checking for,
128-131
resultant cells, 90
Formulas tab, 5
freezing columns/rows, 38
functions, 89
applying cell references
from other work-
sheets, 101-104

arguments
entering, 107
Type argument, 110
Auto-Calculate feature,
104-105
AVERAGE, 91
COUNTA, 94
COUNT function, 94
COUNTIF function, 115
editing, 96-97
FV, 115-117
IF, 110-112
Insert Function com-
mand, 105-117
MAX, 92
MIN, 93
names, referencing,
100-101
PMT, 107-110
SUMIF113-115
future value of invest-
ments, calculating with
FV function, 115-117
FV function, 115-117

G

General format (numeric
data), 60
graphics
AutoShapes, 154,
158-159
clip art, inserting,
156-157
diagrams, inserting,
163-164
drawing objects,
modifying, 155
drawing tools, 153-155
objects
copying, 169
deleting, 171
formatting, 167-168
moving, 168-169
resizing, 170
pictures, layering, 158

shapes, 154
Smart Art, 161-162
text boxes, 155
WordArt, inserting, 160
gridlines
charts, formatting, 139
printing, 186
grouping data with Merge
and Center command,
66-87
groups, 3, 12

H

headers
editing, 191-192
adding, 190-191
height of inserted objects,
resizing, 170
height of rows,
changing, 69
hidden commands, adding
to Quick Access
Toolbar, 13
hidden elements,
printing, 77
hiding
columns, 44, 78-80
pivot table data,
210-211
rows, 43, 76-78
worksheets, 80-81
Home tab, formatting
charts, 146
horizontal alignment,
changing, 68-69
horizontally arranging
workbooks, 22
horizontally centering
worksheets on a
page, 185
Hotmail, signing into
SkyDrive, 216

I

identifying
circular references,
126-127
errors, 118
IF function, 110-112
incorrect source data in
charts, locating, 137
Increase Decimal
command, 58
increasing
column width, 74
decimal places in
numeric data, 61
indenting cell entries,
73-74
inserted page breaks, 182
Insert Function command,
105-117
inserting
AutoShapes, 158-159
clip art, 156-157
columns, 43-44
diagrams, 163-164
objects in worksheets,
164-165
organization charts,
162-171
page breaks, 178-180
pictures from file,
157-158
rows, 42-43
Smart Art, 161-162
WordArt, 160
worksheets in
workbooks, 22
Insert Pictures task pane,
156-171
Insert tab (Ribbon), 4
italic formatting, applying,
65-66
Items in the Workbook
option (SkyDrive), 219

J-K

keyboard shortcuts, 19,
227-230

L

landscape orientation,
184-185
largest cell amount,
calculating, 92
layering pictures, 158
layout of pivot tables,
changing, 205
Layouts gallery, 164
legal size paper, changing
to letter size, 183
legends
adding to charts, 150
formatting, 151
letter size paper, changing
to legal size, 183
limitations of Excel Web
App, 221
loan payments, calculat-
ing with PMT function,
107-110
locating
data, 46
incorrect source data in
charts, 137
logical test functions, performing with IF function,
110-112
lost passwords,
recovering, 27

M

managing
cell comments, 50-51
overlapping
pictures, 158

workbooks
*with Backstage
view, 15*
from SkyDrive, 224
margins, adjusting, 177-178
MAX function, 92
Merge and Center
command, 66-67
MIN function, 93
minimizing the Ribbon, 7
modifying
drawing objects, 155
object properties, 165
mouse wheel, zooming in
with, 34
moving
AutoShapes, 159
charts, 136
data, 44-45
inserted objects, 166
objects, 168-169
objects to another
worksheet, 169
Quick Access Toolbar, 11
versus copying, 26
versus cutting and
pasting, 45
worksheets within
workbooks, 24
multiple email recipients,
sending to, 223
multiple objects,
selecting, 166
multiple workbooks,
viewing onscreen, 20

N

name of fonts, finding, 54
names (functions)
assigning to ranges, 99
referencing, 100-101
natural versus inserted
page breaks, 182
new workbooks,
creating, 16

Number format, 61
number of cells,
counting, 94
numeric data
Accounting format, 62
clearing formatting,
74-76
commas, adding, 58
converting to
percentages, 59
Currency format, 62
Date format, 63
formatting, 58-64
Number format, 61
Text format, 64
Time format, 64
General format, 60
moving, 44-45
replacing, 47
sorting, 49-50
numeric format, applying
to charts, 139
to pivot tables, 207-208

O

objects
copying, 169
deleting, 171
formatting, 167-168
inserting in worksheets,
164-165
moving, 166-169
properties,
modifying, 165
resizing, 170
Online Pictures button,
156-171
Open dialog box, 16
opening
Format dialog box,
168-171
workbooks, 16
workbooks from
SkyDrive, 220
order of operation, 96

organization charts,
inserting, 162-171
orientation
of cells, changing, 71
of paper, selecting,
184-185
Outline form layout (pivot
tables), 205
overlapping pictures,
arranging, 158
overwriting, cells, 123

P

Page Break Preview
button, 176
Page Break Preview view,
183-184
page breaks
adding rows as, 180
inserting, 178-180
natural versus inserted
page breaks, 182
removing, 182, 184
Page Layout tab (Ribbon), 5
page margins, adjusting,
177-178
Page Setup dialog box,
entering specific margins,
178-192
paging through Print
Preview, 174
paper size, changing, 183
password protecting
workbooks, 26-27
passwords
recovering, 27
worksheets,
unprotecting, 29
pasting data, 36-37
percentages, converting
numeric data to, 59
Percent Style command, 59
persistent Format Painter
mode, enabling, 83
Picture button, 157

pictures, inserting from file, 157-158

Picture Tools Format tab, 157-171

pivot tables
areas of, 195
creating, 196-199
data
adding, 204-205
hiding, 210-211
refreshing, 203-204
default location for, 197
dragging fields to other areas, 201
field names, customizing, 206-207
filters, clearing, 211
layout, changing, 205
numeric format, applying, 207-208
rearranging, 199-201
report filter, adding, 201-203
sorting, 211-213
summary calculations, changing, 209-210

PivotTable Tools contextual tab, 204

plot area (charts)
background color, changing, 143
formatting, 142-144

PMT function, 107-110

portrait orientation, 184-185

precedents, 128-131

print area
clearing, 176-192
displaying with Page Break Preview view, 181-182

Print Area command, 176-192

print area, setting, 175-176

printing
cell comments, 187
cell error indicators, 188
centering worksheets on a page, 185
charts, 142-151
column headers, 186
footers, adding, 190-191
gridlines, 186
headers, adding, 190-191
hidden elements, 77
landscape orientation, 184-185
margins, adjusting, 177-178

Page Break Preview view, 181-182

page breaks
inserting, 178-180
natural versus inserted page breaks, 182
removing, 180-182

portrait orientation, 184-185

print area
clearing, 176-192
displaying with Page Break Preview view, 181-182

print area, setting, 175-176

Quick Print command, adding to Quick Access toolbar, 192

repeating titles, 186, 189

returning worksheets to default scale, 183

row headers, 186

rows, adding as page breaks, 180

scale of worksheets, changing, 182-192

worksheets, 191

printing options, Backstage view, 173

Print Preview, 174
displaying, 174
page margins, adjusting, 177-178

zooming in worksheets, 175

properties of objects, modifying, 165

proportionally resizing objects, 170

protecting worksheets, 28

publishing workbooks to the web, 218-219

Q

Quick Access Toolbar, 3, 10
commands
adding, 11-12
removing, 13
groups, adding, 12
hidden commands, adding, 13
moving, 11
Quick Print command, adding, 192

Quick Print command, adding to Quick Access toolbar, 192

R

ranges
conditional sums, 113-115
names, deleting, 101
names, assigning, 99

rearranging pivot tables, 199-201

recognizing circular references, 126-127

recovering
deleted files from SkyDrive, 225
lost passwords, 27

references, checking for, 128-131

referencing names in a function, 100-101

refreshing pivot table data, 203-204

removing
borders, 73
commands from Quick Access Toolbar, 13
data filter drop-downs, 48
page breaks, 180-182
split bars, 39

renaming worksheets, 23

repeating columns headings, 189

repeating titles, printing, 186, 189

replacing data, 47

report filter, adding to pivot tables, 201-203

repositioning
charts, 136
objects, 166, 168-169

resizing
AutoShapes, 159
objects, 170

resultant cells, 90

Review tab (Ribbon), 6

Ribbon, 3
dialog launchers, 4
groups, 3
minimizing, 7
Orientation command, 185
Quick Access toolbar, 3
tabs, 3
Data tab, 5
Formulas tab, 5
Home tab, 4
Insert tab, 4
Page Layout tab, 5
Review tab, 6
View tab, 6

rotating cells, 71

rows
adding as page breaks, 180
deleting, 42-43
fitting content of, 69
freezing, 38
headers, printing, 186
height of, changing, 69
hiding/unhiding, 43, 76-78
inserting, 42-43
references, 7-9
repeating titles, printing, 189

Rows area (pivot tables), 195

S

saving workbooks, 17, 218-219

scale of worksheets, changing, 182-183

security
password protecting workbooks, 26-27
worksheets, unprotecting, 29

selecting
multiple objects, 166
orientation of paper, 184-185
specific cells for calculation, 91

setting the print area, 175-176

shapes
AutoShapes, 154, 158-159
color, applying, 154
styles, applying, 154

sharing workbooks with SkyDrive, 223

shortcut keys, 227-230
Alt+Tab toggle, switching between open workbooks, 19
AutoSum calculation, 90-131

signing into SkyDrive, 217-218

signing up for SkyDrive, 215

size of fonts, changing, 54-55

SkyDrive
deleted files, recovering, 225
Excel Web App, limitations of, 221
Items in the Workbook option, 219
new folders, creating, 219
registering for, 215
signing into, 217-218
visibility of workbook objects, controlling, 219
workbooks
downloading, 222
managing, 224
opening, 220
saving, 218-219
sharing, 223

smallest cell amount, calculating with MIN function, 93

Smart Art, 161-162

SmartArt Tools Format tab, 162

sorting
data, 49-50
pivot tables, 211-213

source data, updating charts, 147-149

source data range (charts), changing, 137

specific margins, entering (Page Setup dialog box), 178-192

splitting worksheets, 39

styles
applying to shapes, 154
customizing, 84-85

SUMIF function, 113-115

summary calculations, changing in pivot tables, 209-210

switching between open workbooks, 18-19

switching between open worksheets, 20

T

tables

data filters, applying, 48

Format as Table feature, 81-82

tabs, 3

coloring, 23

Contextual tabs, 9-10

Data tab, 5

File tab, 6

Formulas tab, 5

Home tab, 4

Insert tab, 4

Page Layout tab, 5

Picture Tools Format tab, 157-171

Review tab, 6

SmartArt Tools Format tab, 133, 162

View tab, 6, 181-182

Tabular form layout (pivot tables), 205

text

converting numeric data to, 64

copying, 36-37

editing, 33

formatting, clearing, 74-76

horizontal alignment, changing, 68-69

indenting, 73-74

pasting, 36-37

replacing, 47

WordArt, inserting, 160

wrapped text, aligning, 72

text boxes, 155

Text format, 64

Time format, 64

titles, printing, 189

troubleshooting

circular references, 126-127

#DIV/0! error, 119-120

error, 59

#NAME? error, 122-123

#REF! error, 124-126

#VALUE! error, 122-124

turning off Auto-Calculate feature, 105

Type argument, 110

typing mistakes, correcting, 32, 35

U

underline formatting, 65-87

undoing deletions, 171

Undo/Redo Stack, 35-51

unhiding

columns, 78-80

rows, 76-78

worksheets, 80-81

unmerging cells, 67

unprotecting worksheets, 29

updating chart source data, 147-149

user interface, 3

V

Values area (pivot tables), 195

vertical alignment, changing, 70

vertically arranging workbooks, 22

vertically centering worksheets on a page, 185

viewing

multiple workbooks onscreen, 20

print area with Page Break Preview view, 181-182

View tab (Ribbon), 6, 181-182

visibility of workbook objects, controlling with SkyDrive, 219

W

width

of columns, fitting to content, 56

of inserted objects, resizing, 170

Windows Taskbar, switching between open workbooks, 18-19

WordArt, inserting, 160

workbooks, 7-8, 15

arranging, 20-22

closing, 17

creating, 16

downloading from SkyDrive, 222

managing

with Backstage view, 15

from SkyDrive, 224

opening, 16, 220

password protecting, 26-27

saving, 17

sharing with SkyDrive, 223

switching between, 18-19

worksheets

adding, 8

copying, 25-26

deleting, 22

inserting, 22
moving, 24
worksheets, 7, 15
  cell comments,
    printing, 187
  cell error indicators,
    printing, 188
  centering on a
    page, 185
  charts, moving, 136
  column references, 8
  columns
    freezing, 38
    headers, adding,
     190-191
    hiding/unhiding,
     78-80
  copying between
    workbooks, 25-26
  deleting from
    workbooks, 22
  diagrams, inserting,
    163-164
  footers
    adding, 190-191
    editing, 191-192
  Format as Table feature,
    81-82
  headers, editing,
    191-192
  hidden elements,
    printing, 77
  hiding/unhiding, 80-81
  inserting in
    workbooks, 22
  landscape orientation,
    184-185
  moving within
    workbooks, 24
  name references, 103
  objects, moving to
    another
    worksheet, 169
  objects, inserting,
    164-165
  page breaks
    inserting, 178-180
    removing, 180-182

  portrait orientation,
    184-185
  print area, setting,
    175-176
  printing, 182-183, 191
  protecting, 28
  renaming, 23
  returning to default
    scale, 183
  row references, 9
  rows
    adding as page
     breaks, 180
    freezing, 38
  scale of, changing,
    182-183
  SmartArt, inserting,
    161-162
  splitting, 39
  switching between, 20
  tabs, coloring, 23
  unprotecting, 29
  zooming in, 34
wrapping data in a cell, 72

X-Y-Z

zooming in worsheets, 34,
  174-175

CHECK OUT MUST-HAVE BOOKS IN THE BESTSELLING MY... SERIES

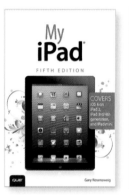

ISBN 13: 9780789750334 ISBN 13: 9780789749482 ISBN 13: 9780789751133 ISBN 13: 9780789748829

Full-Color, Step-by-Step Guides

The "My..." series is a visually rich, task-based series to help you get up and running with your new device and technology, and tap into some of the hidden, or less obvious, features. The organized, task-based format allows you to quickly and easily find exactly the task you want to accomplish, and then shows you how to achieve it with minimal text and plenty of visual cues.

Visit quepublishing.com/mybooks to learn more about the My... book series from Que.

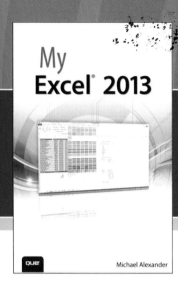

My Excel® 2013

Michael Alexander

Safari Books Online

FREE Online Edition

Your purchase of **My Excel® 2013** includes access to a free online edition for 45 days through the **Safari Books Online** subscription service. Nearly every Que book is available online through **Safari Books Online**, along with thousands of books and videos from publishers such as Addison-Wesley Professional, Cisco Press, Exam Cram, IBM Press, O'Reilly Media, Prentice Hall, Sams, and VMware Press.

Safari Books Online is a digital library providing searchable, on-demand access to thousands of technology, digital media, and professional development books and videos from leading publishers. With one monthly or yearly subscription price, you get unlimited access to learning tools and information on topics including mobile app and software development, tips and tricks on using your favorite gadgets, networking, project management, graphic design, and much more.

Activate your FREE Online Edition at informit.com/safarifree

STEP 1:   Enter the coupon code: NLKCWFA.

STEP 2:   New Safari users, complete the brief registration form.
Safari subscribers, just log in.

If you have difficulty registering on Safari or accessing the online edition,
please e-mail customer-service@safaribooksonline.com